SORTI OUT BELIEVING

Ω

Not Alpha but Omega

:

an alternative guide

Michael Taylor

First Published 2011

Michael Taylor has asserted his right to be
identified as the author of this book.

ISBN 978-0-9551859-3-9

Open House
Publications
Printed and bound in Great Britain by
CPI Antony Rowe, Chippenham and Eastbourne
openhousepublications@talktalk.net

CONTENTS

INTRODUCTION

I often meet and talk with people whose Christian faith and churchgoing are in serious difficulties. They are reluctant to abandon Christianity altogether, but if they are to go on with it they need a different and, for them, a more satisfactory way of doing so. What follows has such people very much in mind.

It does not try to escape being rather personal because I recognise in those I meet a good deal of myself. Over many years now I have engaged from time to time in refining my faith, casting doubt on some of its most easily targeted tenets, adjusting it to challenges from without and within, criticising its institutional expressions, joining with others in trying to renew the church, secularising the gospel, relativising Christianity alongside other faiths, and generally bringing it, as I thought, `up to date`, until these days there is precious little left of what as a young theological student I firmly believed in. So the journey of becoming increasingly doubtful about faith without ever giving it up (or, let it be said, finding the journey `distressing`, however important it was and still is to me) is as familiar to me as to others.

What I have written is also rather personal because it studiously avoids commending an alternative, `more believable`, version of the Christian faith to others or suggesting what others should believe. Instead it sets out what is still meaningful about Christianity to me and, at greater length, some of the thinking about believing that has gone on in my head whilst arriving at it or holding on to it. It describes an alternative way of believing without implying it is the way (and certainly not the destination) for everyone or indeed anyone else at all, in the hope that it may be of some help to others in finding their own.

This refusal to claim too much is not born of modesty or a self-protective instinct for avoiding bold claims and not leaving myself wide open to criticism. It is born of an attempt to be true to one of the central convictions that underlies this book. From one

4

perspective it can sound rather daunting. Whilst no-one will pursue their believing alone if they are wise, or confine its relevance to purely private affairs, it nevertheless remains an intensely private and personal matter because, at the end of the day, we have to take responsibility for it ourselves. From another perspective it can sound rather liberating. No-one else can dictate to us what we should believe. They may be older and wiser and deserve a hearing but, for reasons we shall discuss, they are not in a position to have the final say. This book may be of use in sorting out your believing, indeed I hope it will be since my intentions are constructive, but it cannot presume to suggest what you should believe.

I have tried to write with what intellectual honesty and rigour I can muster whilst avoiding unduly difficult or technical language. I could imagine these pages as `an alternative guide to believing`: an Omega Course for example (see the Appendix) rather than an Alpha Course, complementing rather than opposing an approach which has won the hearts and minds of so many. It starts, for example, with people who are familiar with the Christian community rather than those coming to it as new believers and, second, it reverses perceptions about solid rock and shifting sand. For me, all we have to build on as a basis for our beliefs is our experience of the ever-changing world about us and within us and what we make of it in the company of others, rather than any privileged or `revealed` information which can firmly put an end to our struggles to understand.

I HARD TO BELIEVE

In the last chapter of this book I shall explain why I still go to church every Sunday. Here, at the outset, I need to register the extent of my problems with believing when I do, and faith, for whatever reason, becomes more self-conscious and articulate than the rather undefined but supportive ambience that tends to surround my daily life.

My difficulties with faith are hard to pin down in a word like `unbelief`. At times, especially in settings of overwhelming inspiration, they can virtually disappear. At others, and not infrequently, they give rise to a sense of alienation from the believing community. I am unable, or find it very hard, to believe what I assume others believe and the tradition I belong to expects me to believe. Sometimes the same difficulties can feel like an unresolved dispute between a heart that warms to much in the spirituality of the Christian tradition and a cooler head that insists that, when I think hard, it doesn't add up for me.

In this chapter, which some may prefer to ignore, I give some indication of what I find hard to believe when taking part in a Sunday service and my difficulties are at their most self-conscious and acute.

Leaving aside what the preacher has to say, there are four expressions of the Christian faith which, when I go to church, I'm constantly invited to read, say or sing: the Bible (or the lectionary passages), the words of the service book or liturgy, the creeds, and the hymns; and when I do I often find myself thinking: `I don't agree with that`.

Sometimes it's of relatively little consequence because I'm not being asked to agree with what is being said or sung: that the world was made in seven days for example or that Christ's return and the end of the world are imminent. They were ideas generally accepted a long time ago. Some may still hold to them but most

6

contemporary believers do not. The world has moved on and there is no particular pressure on us to believe them any more.

At other times the disagreements may not be quite so easily set aside - over our sexuality for example or the role of women. The ideas are not merely archaic. They are relevant to the modern world and touch on issues which remain important. Many Christians believe them still and, if challenged, probably believe that I should believe them too. So I am now being asked to agree, at least by some contemporary Christians. However it seems clear that both those who agree and those who do not remain within the Christian community despite the tensions between them, so these are not quite resigning matters.

Of course there will be differences of opinion as to whether a belief falls into the first (`archaic`) or the second (`not a resigning matter`) of my two categories. Some may even judge that some beliefs, which for me fall into the second category, such as belief in the Virgin Birth or in healing miracles or in biblical inspiration, fall into a third which is the one that concerns me here and which might be dubbed `sine qua non` (indispensable). Here we are dealing with beliefs which seem so central and essential to Christianity that without them Christian faith no longer really exists. If you don't or can't believe them, you must surely admit in all honesty that you are no longer a Christian believer. They are resigning matters. Having read through much of the lectionary, prayer books and service books, the creeds and the hymnbook, I have organised these unbeliefs under seven headings. What follows is not an attempt to explain my unbelief (that comes later) and certainly not to justify it, only at this juncture to describe or `confess` it especially when it ceases to be optional, debatable or peripheral and is generally regarded as central to the Christian faith.

1. Another World

The belief in another world is so endemic to Christianity that it is scarcely worth quoting examples but, just to underline the point, it is implicit in a belief in a Creator God, in the pre-existence of Jesus Christ, in the Incarnation and Ascension, in the coming of the Spirit, in the Second Coming, in Judgment, Heaven and Hell, in the general Resurrection of the dead and the hope of Eternal Life. I recognised my unbelief most personally and acutely when I lost a child and realised that, much as I wanted to see and embrace him again, I could not in all honesty regard the prospect of a reunion as anymore than wishful thinking. I also recognise however a `hard not to believe` factor about another world in a persistent personal anxiety about the reckoning and self-exposure I may well have to face after my own death.

2. Resurrection

Belief or rather unbelief in the Resurrection as described in the Easter stories of the empty tomb, its visitors and subsequent encounters with the Risen Christ, and assumed in all the teaching and witnessing that follows has to do with a `sine qua non` with a vengeance. We have only to read the categorical statement in I Corinthians 15: `if Christ was not raised, then our gospel is null and void...and...your faith has nothing in it` to be clear about that; or its echo in George Woodward's hymn:

> Had Christ, that once was slain,
> Ne`er burst his three-day prison,
> Our faith had been in vain....

It would be dishonest to say I believe in the Resurrection but equally misleading to say I do not and I shall return to it later in this discussion (in chapters II and IV).

(note: I have taken all the biblical quotations from the lectionary passages as printed in The Alternative Service Book 1980)

3. The Divinity of Christ

It may be debatable as to whether the New Testament actually goes so far as to explicitly regard Jesus as God. The many references to his being the Son of the Father for example do not necessarily imply his divinity. It is obviously implicit or assumed however in much that is said and read about him in worship: the stories about his birth, transfiguration and ascension, his miracles and power to forgive sins; in his bearing on the cross and how it demonstrated to others his unique status; in the theological stories as told in John 1, Phil 2 and Col 1 about how one who could claim equality with God humbled himself and came to be with us; in his identification with the Lamb upon the throne; in his role as the Word of God, the image of the Father and the object of worship; and in the references to his `pre-existence` in John, I John and Colossians 1: `Before anything was created, he existed`.

When it comes to the Nicene Creed there is no room for ambiguity:

> We believe in one Lord, Jesus Christ
> The only Son of God,
> Eternally begotten of the Father
> True God from true God
> Begotten, not made....

A great many hymns, particularly though not exclusively those associated with Christmas, are equally clear, including `Hark the herald-angels sing` which hails `the incarnate Deity; `In the bleak mid-winter` where a stable is sufficient for the Lord God Almighty; `Love came down at Christmas` which worships the Godhead; and `O come all ye faithful` where God of God and Light of Light abhors not the Virgin's womb.

My unbelief in the divinity of Christ was publicly expressed some 40 years ago in an address to the national assembly of my church (Baptist). It was encapsulated at the time in the observation that I could not confess that Jesus was God but could say that God was in Christ and that I preferred to see God's active presence in Jesus as different from his presence in all of us as a difference in degree but not in kind. That was certainly regarded by many at the time as a resigning matter!

4. Once for All

Central to Christian faith is belief in the saving work of Christ. There have been many attempts to explain how it came about, reflected in scripture reading and hymnody. One familiar one suggests that men and women have disobeyed God and that the consequences of that disobedience are of a different order from other misdemeanours. It is not only death-dealing, it is death deserving and has to be punished if God, despite his longing to forgive, is to remain morally serious. Apparently however it is possible for someone else to pay the price instead of the actual sinners, but the substitute must be of a completely different order: the absolute opposite in fact to a sinful human being, morally perfect and perfectly obedient to God.

Jesus met those stringent demands. He was obedient unto death. He carried the sins of us all. He died for us and paid the price of sin. Justice was done and seen to be done and all who believe and trust that he has rescued them from a fate worse than death will be forgiven and saved: `God shows his love for us in that while we were yet sinners Christ died for us. Since, therefore, we are justified by his blood, much more shall we be saved by him from the wrath of God` (Romans 5), for `in Christ our release is secured and our sins are forgiven through the shedding of his blood` (Ephesians 1).

This `theory of Atonement` as it is sometimes referred to, shines through Philipp Bliss` hymn: `Man of sorrows`:
> Bearing shame and scoffing rude,
> In my place condemned he stood;
> Sealed my pardon with his blood;
> Alleluia! What a saviour!

10

Guilty, vile and helpless we;
Spotless Lamb of God was he:
Full atonement - can it be?
Alleluia! What a Saviour!

And it is more than celebrated by Fanny Crosby in `To God be the glory! Great things he hath done`.

Another quite different explanation of how salvation came about focuses on the distance which has opened up between us and God because of our sin. It talks about ways in which that gap is bridged and enemies are reconciled. One striking image, which we referred to when looking at the divinity and pre-existence of Christ, pictures God, in the person of the Son, becoming human through a process of self-humbling and incarnation: condescension in the best sense! He crosses the divide, takes on our flesh and becomes like we are, even to the extent of experiencing every aspect of human experience, as a result of which we can once again be at-one with God.

This image is simply and beautifully evoked in the prayer after Communion which gives thanks to the Father: `that when we were still far off you met us in your Son and brought us home`.

The book of Hebrews (2 and 4) brings many of these ideas together (including sacrifice, the perfection of Jesus, his being made like us and tempted as we are) round another image, this time of the faithful High Priest who enters the presence of God to offer gifts on our behalf.

Not everything about these explanations is hard for me to believe as we shall see later, and when it comes to ideas, like animal sacrifice, which were compelling at the time but may not be so convincing now, there is no great crisis of faith when new ideas and images have to be substituted for old. What I find hard to believe however is that one single act in time, like the death of an innocent man trading his life for others, or the coming of a child as flesh of our

11

flesh, can fundamentally and irrevocably alter the fate of all of us for all time.

References to this `once-for-all` transaction are constantly made in worship. The great Eucharistic (or Communion) Prayer of thanksgiving for example remembers `his offering of himself made once for all upon the cross`. Hebrews 9 describes how Christ `has entered the sanctuary once and for all, taking with him not the blood of goats and bull calves, but his own blood.` I Peter uses the same phrase: `Christ also died for our sins once and for all`. 2 Corinthians 5 describes how `one man died for all and therefore all mankind has died`. And William Bright, in the words of his Communion hymn, invites us to remember what God has done for us:

> And now, O Father, mindful of the love
> that bought us, once for all, on Calv`rys tree
> and having with us him that pleads above,
> we here present, we here spread forth to thee
> that only off`ring perfect in thine eyes,
> the one true, pure, immortal sacrifice.

5. Victory

Another striking claim is constantly made about the achievements of Jesus. Some regard it as the classic attempt to describe his saving work. The cross above all, but also his ministry and passion, are seen as a battle field where in the end he faces his enemies entirely alone. Ranged against him are those who opposed him during his life including the rulers of the Jews, the Roman occupying forces, the fickle crowds here today and gone tomorrow, even his friends and followers, though more through weakness than malice. But these historical actors are only a front as it were for far more serious foes that have to be reckoned with not on the tiny stage of Palestine but in a cosmic drama.

These foes are variously named as the powers of this world: Sin, Death and the Evil One. They have all of us, past, present and future, in their grip and are now out to make Jesus another of their captives, tempting him to disobey God. But they don't succeed and Jesus, by his faithful obedience even unto death, turns the tables on them. What looks like a disaster, when his enemies apparently get their way and nail him to a cross, is in fact a victory. Jesus triumphs over them, tramples them down, rises from death instead of succumbing to it, ascends to the right hand of God and reigns over all things in all his glory. Sin and death are no more. And this is not just a victory for Jesus; it is a victory for us all. The ancient enemies have no more power over us than over Him and we need not fear them anymore: `death no longer has dominion over him` and `sin will have no more dominion over you` (Romans 6).

Colossians 2 paints a picture of Christ's victory and the humiliation of his enemies in terms of a familiar sight in the ancient world following a successful military expedition: `On that cross he discarded the cosmic powers and authorities like a garment; he made a public spectacle of them and led them as captives in his triumphal procession`.

The Easter Collect speaks of Jesus overcoming the old order of sin and death, and hymn after hymn celebrates Christ's victory. Here are three:

> Love's redeeming work is done
> Fought the fight, the battle won   (Charles Wesley)

> Sing my tongue, the glorious battle,
> Sing the ending of the fray;
> Now above the cross, the trophy,
> Sound the loud triumphant lay:
> Tell how Christ, the world's Redeemer,
> As a victor won the day.   (Venantius Fortunatus)

13

> Up from the grave he arose
> With a mighty triumph o`er his foes   (Robert Lowry)

The same sense of once-for-allness which runs through accounts of our salvation pervades this story about the Victorious Christ, added to which is the claim that the destructive forces which ruin our lives, referred to as Sin and Death, are broken reeds. Both are hard to believe. I suppose they have seemed especially preposterous ideas to me when set against the widespread conflict and destitution, often referred to as `world poverty`, which has formed the background of a good deal of my working life, together with the bloody history of the last two centuries when the forces of death and destruction have seemed no less virulent than before Christ died. Maybe it was similar doubts which inspired Lewis Henley not to celebrate victory but to long for it:

> Thy Kingdom come, O God,
> Thy rule, O Christ, begin;
> Break with thine iron rod
> The tyrannies of sin.
>
> When comes the promised time
> That war shall be no more,
> And lust, oppression, crime
> Shall flee thy face before?

6. The Crucial Decision

When I go to church a great deal of emphasis is placed on what God has done and is doing for me, especially through Jesus Christ; but quite a lot of emphasis is also put on what I need to do for God. Much of it has to do with how I should live my life in response to God's goodness and mercy, in other words it's about Christian discipleship; but some of it refers to a requirement which is much more fundamental and without which there is little point in all the rest. It is not a difficult thing to do and everyone, including me, is perfectly capable of doing it, or so it is said. I must believe in Jesus Christ and what he has done for me. I must repent, have faith and put my trust in him, otherwise I am going to completely miss out on all the benefits that flow from the death and resurrection of Jesus. My sins will not be forgiven. I will remain unreconciled to God. I will go on being in slavery to evil and temptation. Death will remain my greatest enemy and life after death, if you can call it life, will be grim.

John makes the point both positively: `If a man has faith in me...if dead he will live, if alive shall never die` (John 11), and negatively: `he who does not believe is condemned already, because he has not believed in the name of the only Son of God` (John 3). Paul is adamant (2 Corinthians 4) that the only people who find the gospel veiled and difficult are those on the way to perdition: `Their unbelieving minds...make them blind to the light. ` In Acts (17) immediate repentance is the only way to escape judgment. In the Gospels those who refuse the invitation are excluded from the feast of the Kingdom (Luke 14) and those who do not welcome the good news of the Kingdom will find it is `more bearable for Sodom on the great Day than for (that town)` them. (Luke 10)

These stark warnings may not feature prominently in the church's hymns since by definition they are usually sung by those who are assumed to be on the right side of the crucial decision. The warnings are there nevertheless. Julia Howe's frightening vision of the coming of the Lord (`Mine eyes have seen the glory`) accompanied by fateful lightening and a terrible swift sword makes clear that:

> He is sifting out all human hearts
> before his judgment seat.

It goes on to offer this advice:

> O be swift my soul to answer him,

be jubilant my feet!
Our God is marching on.

Christopher Idle (in 'God of all human history') is clear about the need for a decision and its consequences:

God of the present moment
requiring our decision,
now is the hour of judgment
for ruin or salvation.

And an old 17th Century Latin hymn, whilst struggling for the right motive, is equally clear about the fate of those who do not decide for Christ:

My God, I love thee, not because
I hope for heav'n thereby,
nor yet because who love thee not
are lost eternally.

It is hard to believe that any decision for Christ could be as simple and feasible as it is made out to be, or as obligatory, or as crucial, and even harder to believe that there could be such a categorical difference between those who live and die 'in the faith' (to use the words of the liturgy in the prayers for the dead) and those who do not.

7. Global Christianity

There are at least three ways in which I hear Christianity making global claims when I go to church. First, out of all of history, past present and future, Jesus is the only Redeemer. He is the one true light of all; the only way to the Father; the Word of God. There is no salvation apart from him. He brooks no rivals. In the words of the liturgy:

For you alone are the Holy One,

16

you alone are the Lord,
you alone are the Most High.

Peter, preaching soon after Pentecost (Acts 4) agrees: `There is no salvation in anyone else at all, for there is no other name under heaven granted to me, by which we may receive salvation`. Sparrow-Simpson's hymn says the same:

All for Jesus - all for Jesus,
This our song shall ever be:
For we have no hope, nor Saviour,
If we have not hope in thee.

All such sentiments of course find their justification in John 14: `I am the way; I am the truth and I am life; no one comes to the Father except by me`.

The second global claim made by Christianity is that its Gospel, with Christ at its centre, is for all men and women. It is not only the only truth; it is the truth that will save everyone. It is a universal Gospel. More than one collect or short prayer for that particular Sunday (for Epiphany and Pentecost 21 for example) look to the time when all the nations and the whole created order will worship at Christ's feet, and one of the prayers after Communion (`Father of all, we give you thanks and praise..`) asks for steadfastness: `so we and all your children shall be free, and the whole earth live to praise your name`.

Several New Testament passages (see for example Colossians 1 and Ephesians 1) speak of God's intention to redeem the whole world through Christ and in John 10 Jesus speaks about those other sheep he must bring in until there is one flock and one shepherd.

This global mission of the church is vividly pictured in Charles Oakley's hymn: Hills of the north rejoice, with its concluding lines:

Lo from the north they come,

17

From east and west and south:
In Jesus all shall find their rest,
In him the universe blest.

Other hymns send the church out to fulfil its global task:

Go forth and tell!
O Church of God, awake!
God's saving news
to all the nations take:
proclaim Christ Jesus,
Saviour, Lord and King,
that all the world
his worthy praise may sing   (James Seddon)

and again:

Lift high the cross, the love of Christ proclaim
Till all the world adore his sacred name (Kitchin and Newbolt)

The third global claim made by Christianity is that its mission to all the nations will be successful either in this world or the next. Christ's winning ways will draw everyone unto himself and unite all things on earth and in heaven. Eventually, beyond history maybe, there will be a new heaven and a new earth together with a new city devoid of all suffering into which all the nations will gather though not, it has to be said, those whose ways are false or foul (Revelation 21). Paul (in Romans 8) looks forward to the time when `the creation itself will be set free from its bondage to decay and obtain the glorious liberty of the children of God`, and both scripture and hymnody are confident that `At the name of Jesus, every knee shall bow` (Caroline Noel following Philippians 23).

Sometimes a more daring note is struck by suggesting that this vision will be realised here on earth. Arthur Ainger's hymn: `God is working his purpose out as year succeeds to year`, is perhaps the most obvious but by no means the only example of it:

> Nearer and nearer draws the time,
> the time that shall surely be,
> when the earth shall be filled
> with the glory of God
> as the waters cover the sea.

Looking back over these three global claims, I find it hard to believe that the only truth of a saving or life-enhancing nature is to be found in Christ so that he has global supremacy on that score. Again, whilst the Gospel may strike a generous, universal and all-inclusive note about, say, God's love and welcome for everyone, I don't believe that the church has the ability to bring the entire world to Christ however hard it tries to win it over, or that history will ever come to such a satisfactory conclusion that it could be described as `heaven on earth` or `a new heaven and a new earth`. Looking beyond history, I have already confessed to difficulties about believing in some grand resolution of all our earthly struggles in another world.

8. The Presence of Christ

I assume that talk of the work of Providence and of the Holy Spirit in our lives and references to Jesus as a constant companion and continuing presence amount, in practice, to much the same thing. This is God with us, indwelling, strengthening, comforting, protecting and guiding us at every moment of our lives. This is what John 14 seems to promise with its talk of Jesus not leaving the disciples but coming back to make a home with them and of them dwelling in him and he in them as the vine and its branches; and this is what is asked for in the collect for Christmas Day: `Grant that, as we are born again in him, so he may continually dwell in us`. The same request is found in many a hymn of which the most well-known and popular is probably Francis Lyte's: `Abide with me`; the most sentimental: Walter Mathams` `Jesus friend of little children, Be a friend to me`; and one of the oldest: St Patrick's Breastplate:

> Christ be with me, Christ within me,
> Christ behind me, Christ before me.
> Christ beside me, Christ to win me,
> Christ to comfort and restore me.

Very often in worship this presence is spoken of as if it has been granted and we now enjoy the company of Jesus in much the same way as two disciples enjoyed it on the road to Emmaus (Luke 24), walking and talking along the way. Joseph Scriven`s `What a friend we have in Jesus` is a good example of this but the most obvious is A.H.Ackley`s rousing chorus:

> He lives, he lives, Christ Jesus lives today!
> He walks with me and talks with me along life's narrow way.

The Eucharist or Holy Communion has been the subject of a good deal of controversy not least over what exactly becomes of the bread and wine when it is set aside or consecrated for this special meal. There is general consensus however that it is a more formal and ritualistic way of not only `remembering` Christ's death and resurrection but `realising` his presence with us now. Apart from asserting that we eat the flesh and drink the blood of Christ at Holy Communion, and do so in the presence of the divine Majesty, the words of the liturgy are somewhat reticent on this point. Some communion hymns are less so:

> Come, risen Lord and deign to be our guest;
> nay, let us be thy guests; the feast is thine;
> thyself at thine own board make manifest,
> in thine own sacrament of bread and wine.

> we meet, as in that upper room they met;
> thou at thy table, blessing, yet dost stand   (George Briggs)

It is not difficult to understand and accept that `pretending` or `imagining` that Jesus is still with us, side by side as it were, can be a helpful devotional practice, but I find it hard to believe that it bears any relation to reality.

....

This catalogue of disagreements and unbeliefs, taken by itself, is in danger of painting far too negative a picture and leaving the impression that when I go to church I spend the whole of my time dissenting from what is being said or sung. By way of restoring the balance, and again without at this stage trying to explain or justify anything, here are some prominent aspects of worship which rarely provoke any sense of disagreement at all.

The Psalms are regularly said or sung in most churches. Taken as a whole they are a wonderful collection of human sentiments. `All human life is here` - or nearly all. They express gratitude for the good things of life. They wonder at a vast and incomparable world. They delight in nature. They know about suffering, defeat and humiliation. They complain about hardships and protest at injustice. They don't hide their hostilities and prejudices. They can be self-righteous in tone as well as self-critical. They long for safety. And however bad things get there is an irrepressible optimism about the future: things will get better. Almost all of these sentiments are readily recognisable as my own and not only provide an insight into how the Psalmists and those who originally sang their songs felt about their lives but also give me an opportunity to express and reflect on how I feel about mine.

Many of the hymns we now sing in church are problematic, as we have seen, because they are full of references to highly developed core Christian teaching with which I am expected to agree. In that respect they are unlike the Psalms but in other respects they are very similar. Through them we express our gratitude and wonder, our fears and sorrows, our failure and aspirations, and our hopes for better and more peaceful times to come.

21

Both Old and New Testaments contain a great deal of teaching: moral, spiritual, social, even psychological (such as Paul's explorations in Romans 4 and 7) concerning life and how best to deal with it, which seems highly valuable even if at times open to healthy debate.

Retelling history is another prominent feature of a church service. Almost all the Old Testament lessons fall into that category and a good many of the New. Of course there is a high level of potential disagreement when we begin to ask if this or that really happened as it is told, particularly when it comes to details or to the early stories about how the world and history began. But in general I feel no need to distance myself or suspend belief when worship rehearses the great narratives of Israel's growing sense of destiny as she is born out of the risky adventures of her ancestors, suffers famine and hardship, sinks into slavery, escapes oppression, settles in a land of her own, struggles for internal order and justice, experiences varying fortunes as she unites or divides as a nation, prospers or faces defeat, goes into exile, eventually finds her way home again but only to face occupation and decline until she is forced to pin her hopes increasingly on some future deliverer who will rescue her from all the hands of those that hate her and inaugurate some idyllic age when 'the cow and the bear shall be friends' (Isaiah 11)

Neither is there any problem about the way the story continues into the New Testament, especially in the Gospels and the Acts of the Apostles, or about rehearsing it repeatedly when I go to church. Again there will be scepticism about the details but not for me about the story of a man who many, at least initially, welcomed as the hoped for deliverer and others feared and resisted from the start. I have indicated where believing gets difficult though it can be argued that that has more to do with later assessments of the story than the story itself. But a sense of alienation and disbelief does not enter the picture as I hear about how Jesus upheld what was arguably the best in his Jewish tradition, committed himself to

22

the poor and the broken; or about what he did and taught; or as I listen to his parables about talents, justice, generosity of spirit, fairness and kindness, worldly astuteness, neighbourly and parental love, self-righteousness, humility, gratitude, the dangers of being judgmental, and his sayings about anxiety, putting first things first - and last, the narrow gate to life, pecking orders, suffering and hope, and who is blessed.

And unbelief does not enter the picture as I hear about his love of life and his asceticism, his strictures and inclusiveness, and the way he forced a rethink (not out of line with some perceptive teaching in the Old Testament, especially in Isaiah, about a suffering servant) about what sort of deliverer he was and what sort of future his followers would face: hopeful of new beginnings but brought about by costly service and humility rather than worldly dominance and supremacy - strands of a narrative that re-appears in the compelling visions of the book of Revelation.

Above all, I have no sense of unbelief as I hear the great passion narrative, traditionally read in its entirety on Palm Sunday, from the prayers and betrayals in the Garden of Gethsemane to the last breath at the ninth hour.

These for me are credible stories out of which, not surprisingly, great faith traditions have sprung.

Prayers are of course a prominent feature of worship. There are no problems about sharing in the heartfelt yearnings and concerns which they express whether they turn to thanksgiving or confession or supplication or intercession. On the contrary I appreciate and empathise with a good many of them. Take the Anglican collects - at least one for every Sunday of the year. They are beautifully succinct little prayers which often gather up or `collect` together key ideas that run through the lessons for that particular week. For example, on Palm Sunday, the readings focus on Christ's humility and the collect for the day asks that it be a characteristic of our own lives. The collects follow a formula, part of which is highly doctrinal and full of ideas which, as I have said, I find difficult. They almost always refer to the Trinity of God the Father, his Son Jesus Christ and the Holy Spirit together with our redemption through Christ's cross and resurrection, his subsequent glory and our hope of sharing it with him. In other words these prayers unfailingly rehearse core, `sine-qua-non` tenets of the Christian faith so that makes it difficult to make them mine.

On the other hand they frequently refer to realities which I recognise, such as the need for forgiveness or right judgment or safety, and give voice to aspirations which I hope I share such as patience, humility, good desires, the will to serve and a heart fixed `where lasting joys are to be found`. At that level I have no difficulty in making them my own. I have doubts about the wrappings but not about the content, about the doctrinal context of these prayers but not about what is being asked and longed for. Many would argue that the one cannot survive or make sense or have real substance without the other. When I go to church I find, in practice, that it usually does.

II MAKING FAITH FIT

1. One of my earliest problems with religion was trying to make it `fit` with my life. I don't mean the problem of living up to my ideals or being true to what I believed: putting my money where my religious mouth was, as it were. Of course that failure was and remains a problem but it is not the one I am referring to here. The problem was that what my religion told me in an almost descriptive way did not fit very well with my experience. What religion said was the case did not seem to be the case in everyday life. It did not ring as true as it was made out to be by the institutions and people who taught it and passed it on. Let me give some fairly obvious, almost naive, examples.

I was told that my prayers would be answered: ask and it will be given you; seek and you will find; knock and it will be opened to you. At ten years of age I prayed that my father would get better but he died. At seventeen or eighteen I prayed in evangelical mode for the `success` of the first Billy Graham crusade in the UK (in the 50`s) but it failed to stem the tide of secularisation.

Brought up as a Baptist (though with a strong Anglican background and, now, Anglican leanings!), a great deal of importance was placed on my own decision, once I was old enough to be responsible for it, to become a believer and be baptised.

It would mark decisively the end of my old life and the beginning of a new one, following Jesus. I was duly baptised when I was fourteen but it was not long before I had to settle for a life that was much the same as before. I was a committed churchgoer, as I had always been, but I was certainly not, as I had been led to believe I would be, a better one or a very different person. I was confirmed as the person I already was.

Claims that the life, death and resurrection of Jesus made a difference seemed not to fit on a much larger scale than my own personal life. The world was certainly different after his coming. There was a growing movement called Christianity and a growing number of institutions called churches; and history, whether political, economic, social, cultural or moral, would have been quite another story without them. But if the world was different I could not see that on balance it was any better. All the talk about it being redeemed and a new creation replacing the old, did not `fit` with the wars and rumours of war, the crime, poverty, cruelty and suffering which were everywhere around me. Some things got better; other things got worse. The moral tone did not noticeably improve and generally speaking the world seemed as much in need of so-called `redemption` or salvation two thousand years after Christ as it ever did.

A fourth example represents the most enduring sense of `misfit`, not just in my religious journey but in the whole story of Christianity. We are told that Jesus is the most reliable clue to what God is like (the Word made flesh so that we can see for ourselves) and that the word which best sums him, and therefore God, up is `love`. So God being God, in God's dealings with us, love and power come together. God's desire is to love us and God has the power to do so. How is it then that so much of life is blighted by what any loving parent would wish to (and in God's case, could) do away with, from the personal loss and pain that most of us suffer to the disasters inflicted on millions by wind and rain, conflict, disease and drought? The idea that God loves us does not seem to fit the facts.

2.   One response to the problem of `misfit` is to be told, or acknowledge for ourselves as we grow older and wiser, that we misunderstood what we were taught. We learn more about faith as we grow up and come to understand it better. It becomes deeper and more sophisticated rather than naive and juvenile.

We should not feel unduly let down or misled, for example, when God does not give us what we ask for in our prayers. For one thing we might have forgotten that we are expected to pray with faith, believing that God can indeed move mountains; and for another God may well have answered our prayers but not in the way we expected. Perhaps we asked in good faith for what we believed was best: that my father would live and that Billy Graham would convert the whole of England to his robust, evangelical way of life; but maybe God thought otherwise and dealt with our cares and concerns in other, more appropriate and beneficial ways. And sometimes with hindsight, we come to see that God's way, or how things turned out, was in fact for the best.

At fourteen I apparently got the difference that baptism and being a Christian make seriously wrong. For `once born` Christians like me, Baptism is a bit like marriage. It's a matter of `coming out` and going public about what is already true: that two people have developed a relationship and are committed to one another. So that nothing really changes at all. What would be a change would be to break the link rather than confirm it. More importantly perhaps, the difference between Christians and others is not that their lives are lived on a markedly superior moral and spiritual plane. Sometimes quite the reverse is sadly the case and, at best, they continue with their fair share of faults and failings like everyone else. One difference that might be valid however, though here again Christians can be as hung-up and anxious as the rest, is that they recognise their shortcomings but are somewhat relaxed about them because they know that they are forgiven and accepted in spite of them. They take life with its moral and spiritual endeavours seriously but they don't worry too much when they don't deal with it as well as they might. They struggle hard to be more Christlike but when they fail they do not feel disqualified.

That the moral and spiritual quality of human life has not improved since the dawn of Christianity is disputable. Do we not have a more refined sense of human rights for example, even if we don't live up to it? But even if convincing evidence of an overall improvement is hard to come by, as I believe it is, we should not, according to a deeper understanding of our faith, become cynical about the ability of God through Christ to redeem the world. According to Christian teaching it is a long-term strategy which deliberately refuses to force the issue. Wheat and tares will grow together and may only be finally separated out at the end of time. There will be a new, redeemed world but not yet.

According to one vivid image (Oscar Cullman's) from the Second World War the decisive battle has been fought and won. The cross and resurrection is `D-Day`. The devil and all his works have been roundly defeated. His back has been broken. But the aftermath has still to be dealt with and victory celebrations (`V-Day`) will not be in order for some time to come. That is why the Bible talks about the Kingdom of God or God's rule, where God's will is done, as being here but not here yet; as having come with the coming of Jesus but still lying in the future. And that is why the New Testament is full of references to ongoing battles: moral, spiritual, political and cosmic, still to be won. Swift and magical transformation scenes imply a shallow view of personal change and were never on God's agenda.

When it comes to the contradiction between an all-powerful and loving God and the sufferings of what are supposed to be his children, I had to learn that I was pointing the finger in the wrong direction and was forgetting two important facts: one was human freedom and the other was human perversity. The problem does not lie with God. It lies with us. God does everything possible to bear our sorrows and heal our wounds. The clearest indication of that is the lengths God went to once upon a time in Jesus which is typical of the lengths God is prepared to go to through God's spirit all the time. There are two great hindrances however to God's success. One is self-imposed by God and wisely so. We are free to accept or reject the love and healing on offer and our freedom will not be overridden by the lover however powerful. That is partly out of respect for the loved one and partly because imposing this kind of relationship is a contradiction in terms. If it is not the result of a willing response but is merely forced on us, then it is not a healing and sorrow-free relationship at all.

The second and even greater hindrance to God's success however is our human perversity which not only refuses God's loving overtures but seems determined to make matters worse. Even if some disasters are `natural`, much of the poverty in the world is made by us and could be eradicated if we had the will to do so. It is our selfishness that gets in the way. Whilst not all the diseases that ravage our communities are our fault, even if they were, most could be eliminated if only we behaved differently (in our sexual encounters for example) and shared our knowledge and resources, such as medicines, more fairly. Again, if we took care of the earth, the air, the sky, the sea instead of knowingly polluting and over-exploiting them we could control the increasingly negative effects of climate change which will hit the already poor the hardest. What produces an apparent dissonance between the existence of an all-powerful and loving God and the harsh realities of life is not God's perversity but our own. There are rules of the game and boundaries, symbolised by the forbidden fruit of a single tree in an otherwise idyllic garden, and we choose to ignore them.

Here then are a few examples of how the problems of faith can be eased as understanding grows and deepens. It does not necessarily follow of course that they are removed.

3. Another response to the problem of `misfit`, where what my religion tells me does not ring true to experience, is to be made more aware of what I am trying to fit it into. Could it be a case of trying to fit a square peg in a round hole or more appropriately in this particular instance, as we shall see, a round peg in a square hole? And when it doesn't fit, am I raising questions about the peg when perhaps I should be raising questions about the hole? The constant concern that my faith should fit the `facts` is itself rather telling. Am I trying to put faith in a straitjacket and assuming it is always faith that has to give?

As a European I have inherited an intellectual tradition which goes back at least to the 18th century and the Enlightenment. For close on three hundred years it has not been seriously challenged and it is understandable why many of us take it for granted. Far from questioning it, it is so much a part of us - in our blood - that we are scarcely aware of it. In essence it took a radically different view of how we know what is what. Beforehand knowledge was given to us mainly by the church, and its basis was divine authority. To put it crudely, God had revealed the truth about our lives partly through the way he had made the world but mainly through his Son, Jesus Christ, the Bible and the Spirit at work in the church. Wise and holy men in the form of priests and theologians, carefully vetted by the ecclesiastical authorities, studied and interpreted those revelations and handed down their conclusions to their congregations. So they became `matters of fact`. What they said about sin and salvation, heaven and hell, death and resurrection, prayer and miracles, saints and sinners, suffering and punishment, even about wider social and political matters, was true because they had it on good authority and embodied that authority in themselves.

At the Enlightenment (not unrelated to the Reformation) there was not only a rebellion against the heavy-handed ways of the church and its habit of calling the tune on every occasion, but also a reaction against this top-down approach to knowledge. Why not start from the bottom and work upwards, gradually building what we know from careful observation of the world about us and within us? We know what we see and touch, rather than what we are told by God and the church. Knowledge is the result of an inductive process working things out from our experience, not a deductive process from truths coming from nowhere or from `God`. Knowledge is a posteriori not a priori: coming after or in the light of events, not before them.

As a result, the authority of the church as the reliable source of knowledge was replaced by the `authority` of the facts. Valid conclusions would only be drawn after careful observation, moving from particular examples to more general theories which might link them and explain them and help to predict what will happen next.

These theories would remain tentative until checked and rechecked against more and more examples: what we now know as the scientific method.

This long tradition of relying on facts rather than revelations from on high has proved extremely fruitful, vastly expanding our knowledge and transforming the quality of millions of lives. So it is not surprising that it has gained an authoritative status all of its own, and it helps to explain why we become increasingly sceptical about religious claims which do not fit the facts, or which we cannot fit into the facts, and why our European, `modern` mindset causes such difficulties for faith.

Without denying that it should cause difficulties however, and without regressing to blind dependence on authority, is it possible that this whole astonishingly productive approach to knowing is also somewhat blinkered and too ready to rule out of court what won't fit into its own preconceptions? Is it a rather angular, straitened, square hole which cannot accommodate round pegs? Some have asked whether it is a rather masculine rather than feminine way of looking at things. Why for example should we not know things in others ways, through the insights of poets and artists, or the experience of mystics and contemplatives, or our own intuition? What about the knowledge, often of a person, that wins our trust, basing our religion on what as Christians we call `faith` rather than intellectual assent? Why should there not be other dimensions to life besides its measurable height, length, width and depth (the philosopher John Hick refers to: 'The Fifth Dimension`) and why should we not take them seriously? Are we so sure that if a reality cannot be empirically verified - pinned down and pointed to as it were on the ground - that it doesn't exist and has no meaning? Why should miracles and surprises be discounted simply as what we do not yet understand in a scientific sense rather than considered as possible intimations that there may be more to life than is ever dreamed of in a matter-of-fact philosophy? What is the basis for my growing scepticism about another world? Have I been blinded to

31

the evidence? Should we not be wary of ruling out the misfits on the basis of the assumptions and prejudices we bring to them and be prepared instead to allow them to challenge our assumptions? It could even be argued that to do so would keep us in the best `scientific tradition`!

Growing numbers of Christians in Africa and Asia have not been so heavily influenced by the Western intellectual tradition I have been describing. They are not untouched by it and they are certainly not ignorant of it, but it is not in their blood in quite the same way as it is in ours. They easily and eagerly embrace aspects of faith which I find difficult, such as the power of prayer, prophecy as direct guidance from God, healing miracles, exorcism and the workings of the spirit. Maybe in time their beliefs will be eroded by `the facts`. Maybe they have a rather more rounded or holistic hole into which they can more readily fit a round peg.

A second example comes to mind of the need to be aware of the assumptions we bring to our difficulties with faith and to question those assumptions rather than simply question the faith. With the Enlightenment, as we have seen, came an enormous expansion of knowledge. One easily verifiable aspect of that was an astonishingly steep rise in inventions and with inventions came change. New machines not only enabled some people to make money but demanded shifts of population and new patterns of working. Advances in medicine and sanitation turned the tide against diseases that had blighted millions of lives. New methods of transport by water, road and rail, and eventually by air, brought ease of communication and trade and opened up new worlds with their fresh ideas and unthought-of possibilities. On so many fronts life began to get better first for a privileged few but gradually for the majority of the population, at least in Europe and North America. It became only natural to believe in progress; and it is easy to see why the optimism of this new age infected the Christian faith.

As the influence of the Western world spread towards the South, Christian missionaries went with it, and with them went this faith in the decisive life, death and resurrection of Jesus Christ that had dealt a mortal blow to evil and sin and had set in motion a powerful movement inspired by God capable of sweeping across the world and transforming it into the Kingdom of love and peace which God had always had in mind from the very beginning. It is not surprising that Christians learned to sing with conviction:

> Nearer and nearer draws the time,
> The time that shall surely be;
> When the earth shall be filled with the glory of God
> As the waters cover the sea.

Christian believers before the Enlightenment and the changes which science brought about would not have expected the world and the circumstances of their lives to change as a result of their faith. It had always stayed much the same and they had always stayed much the same along with it: rich and poor, high and low, here and there. They had never thought the world would be otherwise. That was the way things were and the way God had made them. The Gospel took care of some of their fears about sin and death and it gave them some hope of a better, brighter world to come. It kept them on the straight and narrow, but it never occurred to them that it had anything to do with `progress`. Their faith helped them to manage the world as it was rather than manufacture a new one.

But we are now conditioned to more or less expect progress. We read the Gospel, not as expecting the imminent end of the world, nor as merely supporting me through this troublesome life until I reach a better life to come, but as the means of making not just scientific progress but moral and spiritual progress as well in this world of yesterday`s, today's and tomorrow's. So somewhat unfairly perhaps, when it dawns on me that all this talk of progress is probably whistling in the wind and that there is little to choose between the bloody 20th century for example and all that went

33

before it, I blame it on my Christian faith and its failure to live up to the expectations it has raised rather than question the mindset that assumes things will get better and better all the time.

Needless to say the relationship between Christian faith and ideas of progress is more complicated than I have made out, not least because some Christian teaching about the equal value of individuals and personal freedom is itself progressive; but the broad point about being prepared to question the assumptions we bring to our doubts about faith, and not just question the faith itself, still holds good.

4. So far I have characterised my problems with Christian faith as `misfits`, where what I am told by faith doesn't square with the facts. I have mentioned two ways of responding to them. The first is to correct any misunderstandings and gain a deeper and more sophisticated appreciation of what is being taught. The second is to be more aware of the assumptions and even prejudices I bring to faith and be prepared to question them. I want now to look in one or two other directions.

To begin with there are problems which arise for faith when we are confronted with new realities or `facts` of which we were previously unaware. They can be resolved, though maybe not for everyone, not by correcting old misunderstandings but by understanding faith in a new way. The obvious example is when we have to reckon with a multi-faith world. It has always been there of course but, until the days of the modern missionary movement and globalisation, previous generations did not have to live with it as we do now. It was not a daily presence in their streets and cities. They were scarcely aware of the extent, history and solidity, let alone possible validity, of any other faith such as Islam, Hinduism, Buddhism or Sikhism out there beyond their far horizons. Judaism was the exception for obvious reasons. Where these other faiths were heard of they were dismissed as invalid and capable of being

34

overcome sooner or later as the Gospel spread. Previous generations were able to sing with complete conviction:

> For the darkness shall turn to the dawning
> And the dawning to noon day bright;
> And God's great Kingdom shall come on earth,
> The Kingdom of love and light.

The perception of a world which, if it was not already Christian, was waiting to become Christian (ripe for the picking) sat easily with the claims of Christianity to be the only true religion and Jesus the only way to the Father, and with the idea that there is no salvation outside of the church.

Today, given our awareness of a multi-faith reality, some still hold fast to those exclusive views. Some acknowledge that other faiths have their insights and achievements but still regard Christianity as superior. Some recognise that, like it or not, we have to live with people of other faiths and respect them whilst remaining confident of the final outcome. Some have attributed all that is good about other faiths to the workings of a hidden, Christlike God and have spoken of 'anonymous Christianity'. Some combine elements of all these responses, all of which fall short of any fundamental shift in their own beliefs.

Some however go further and jettison the belief that Christianity is the only valid religion. Instead, they understand it as one of many ways to find life and God. We travel along different pathways but we are heading for the same destination. This idea is strengthened by recognising what religions have in common: a global ethic for example where all subscribe to the same fundamental moral ideals including love of neighbour. This 'Copernican Revolution' as it has been called (by John Hick), where faiths no longer circle round Jesus but all religions, including Christianity, circle round God, allows us to hold on to a belief in one God (important since if God is God he can hardly have any equals, not to mention rivals) even if that God is perceived in many different and less than perfect ways. It also allows us to hold on to the conviction, very hard to let go of emotionally, that Christianity is still the most important religion for us. We may come to appreciate others but most of us will never come to experience them or `inhabit` them in quite the same way. Our Christianity may well be enriched by other faiths but it remains for us, though quite properly not for everyone else, the way to God.

Another example of understanding faith differently (rather than correcting misunderstandings) does not perhaps strike at the very heart of Christian teaching, about the uniqueness of Christ and his salvation for example, to the same extent as coming to terms with other faiths, but its consequences may be just as important. When science was in its hey-day it demonstrated just how brilliant it was at manipulating the natural world for what appeared to be the benefit of mankind. It could take raw materials like cotton and wool and turn them ever more cheaply into clothes. It could take coal and gas and water and turn them into heat and light and steam. It could take metals, learn the laws of physics and then manufacture engines. It could refine crude oil to give those engines `horse` power. It could mix chemicals to enrich the soil and control pests in order to grow bigger and better crops. In time it even learned to alter the structure of the plants themselves in order to do the same.

And so this arbitrary list could go on; and it all `fitted` very nicely with what God seemed to be saying in some of the earliest passages of the Bible. He had made the good earth for our benefit. He had made us as the crown of is creation. He had put us on earth as if in a garden, and set us to work to make the most of it. The biblical faith and science were at one in this, though they often seemed to be at odds elsewhere. We were meant to subdue the earth, bend it to our purposes and exploit it for our good.

We did not notice, or choose to notice until comparatively recently, that apart from the tensions and inequalities that this inventive and adventurous spirit could cause as one group of pioneers got ahead of another, the good earth was beginning to crack under the strain.

36

Once we did, it gave rise to growing talk of scarce resources, exhausted stocks, pollution of earth and sky, holes in the atmosphere and the dire consequences of global warming. Perhaps the faith had been completely misunderstood, though on second thoughts that seemed unlikely. It doesn't take much imagination to realise what human life would have been like had we never manipulated the natural world at all. Humanity would not have survived. A policy of 'leave well alone' would have meant the death of us. In any case we are an inseparable part of nature and its development. Our very existence along with our needs, like food and shelter for example, make a difference to the planet like it or not. There is no choice as to whether we interfere with, or manipulate, or exploit the earth. We might even say it is not just part of our nature that we do so, but part of nature itself.

It is not that the biblical faith was simply misunderstood by science but that, with an awareness we did not have before, faith has to be understood in a different way. We are not made to conserve the world 'just as it has always been' or too readily assume we have exhausted its capabilities. We are made to develop it, ourselves included, but at the same time to take care of it: to avoid as far as we can making changes that will jeopardise its future (which includes our future and that of our children); to find out more about how one thing affects another in the intricate web of nature's inter-dependency; to discover the difficult balance that exploits the earth without damaging it and so fulfil our calling as stewards and co-creators of a world which can offer fuller and happier but sustainable ways of life for everyone - a calling close to the Islamic understanding of man as God's caliph or representative on earth.

Where faith proves difficult then in the face of new realities it can be understood differently instead of being dismissed.

5. Another rather subtle way of holding on to faith and dealing with its problems is to understand it in such a way that it will fit the facts whatever they are. As a result, it may not be entirely immune to attack but it will certainly be far less vulnerable.

Some approaches to prayer and providence for example allow nothing and no-one to undermine the believer's faith in them. Whatever happens, be it good fortune or bad, all that could be hoped for or deep disappointment, success or disaster, sickness or health, it is all for the best. God's ways are mysterious. God's wisdom is greater than ours. God understands and takes into account what is beyond our knowing. God has the whole wide world in God's hands. Faith here is not based on evidence (not even the highly selective evidence which gives God the glory for all things bright and beautiful but never calls God to account for all things dark and ugly) but rooted in a disposition of trust in God's goodness, come what may.

Teaching about the coming of God's kingdom can be immunised in much the same way. As it becomes 'better understood' it becomes increasingly compatible with the facts, whatever they may be. Any development that seems worthy of approval, such as a temporary peace breaking out, or an increase in the boundaries of the Christian church, or a medical triumph, can be celebrated as a sign that the Kingdom is on its way or that outposts of it have already been established. All the continuing catastrophes and perversities of human life on the other hand can be explained by reminding ourselves that wheat and tares grow together and the final coming of the Kingdom is not yet. Any overwhelming disaster, casting doubts on the final triumph of good over evil, can be met with the assurance that things will get worse before they get better, as forecast by Jesus himself, but the end, and with it God's kingdom, will surely come. There are no facts which can disprove such a scenario.

Another example of this kind of immunity relates to a core Christian belief: that the Gospel has the power to redeem the world and its peoples. We can criticise ourselves for understanding (or misunderstanding) the Gospel too much in terms of modern ideas about progress, as we have seen, but even if such ideas are on the wane we can make the power of the Gospel `fit` whatever happens like a glove. If the Gospel redeems some and not others, that is their choice. If it doesn't make headway like a saving rollercoaster, that is because it respects rather than overrides human freedom. No-one has redemption thrust upon them. If there is a serious roadblock, where once again things get significantly worse rather than better, that is due to the intransigence of wicked men and women or the resurgence of the powers of this world. If it looks as though some people get a better chance to accept Christ than others, because of geography, or culture, or experience, or even mental ability, allowances can be made in the after life. If committed Christians don't always impress us by the moral and spiritual quality of their lives, that is because `justification` or the initial redemptive act which grants us God's forgiveness is not to be confused with `sanctification`, the much longer process which leads to true holiness of life, a process which, according to some, may well go on after death where purgatory becomes the final preparatory school for heaven.

We are no longer dealing with attempts to adjust or re-state our faith to fit the facts. Here is a faith that will fit them whatever they may be. It does not even rely on the evidence of things unseen. Everything that can be seen becomes evidence for faith.

Some Christian beliefs are even more indifferent to the facts. They are immune because they don't really refer to them. Take the divinity of Christ. The facts it might supposedly rest on, like the miracles of Jesus or the resurrection, or the reaction of those present at the time, are no longer available to us to test out one way or the other. But the belief does not really rest on them even if they were. Instead it arises out of the internal logic of faith itself. The reason why Christianity goes beyond saying that Jesus was a deeply impressive and memorable character, for which the evidence seems plentiful, and claims for him the unique status of godly and human perfection is not that the facts support it but that the doctrine of our salvation requires it.

One argument runs something like this. We are to be freed from our sins and their consequences. Because in the end those sins are crimes against God, their consequences are incalculable, stretching into eternity, and the cost of dealing with them is equally great. Old ideas of penal substitution however suggest that someone else can bear that cost. A sacrifice can be made on our behalf, but only by something or someone free from sin. When the sacrifice is for all the enormous sins of mankind it escalates the requirements so that only someone as important and perfect as the Son of God can qualify. He alone can be the lamb without blemish that takes away the sins of the world. Christ's divinity and perfection are the products of a (theo-) logical argument about how redemption works and have little if anything to do with the facts.

6. If however faith is going to be of any interest to me it must be compatible with my experience, which means it cannot ignore or ride above the facts altogether. If faith tries to articulate the truth about my life: what is going on in it and what is its meaning and purpose, then it has to engage not with a fantasy world or with some virtual reality or purely theoretical realm of existence but with what actually seems to be the case in my earthly pilgrimage. There has to be some sort of fit; which leads me finally, in this part of the discussion, to pay homage to what, for me, has been one of the most profound and persuasive accounts of Christian faith that I have come across. It addresses many of my problems even though, in the end, it leaves me not altogether convinced.

It owes much to a German woman called Dorothee Solle and an English priest called W.H.Vanstone (both now dead). It brings together four attractive ideas. The first is captured in the vivid story of the Jews in a concentration camp in the midst of the Holocaust, watching their fellow Jews, including children, being hanged by the Nazis. One Jew turns to the other and understandably asks the age old question (about a God of power and a God of love):`Where is God in all of this? `, to which comes the reply: `He is there, on the gallows, with the rest`. That contradicts any idea that God somehow stands back and orchestrates human suffering as punishment for our sinful disobedience, or at least tolerates it as a necessary consequence, and it goes further than suggesting he merely sympathises and feels for us in our distress, wishing that things didn't have to be this way. Rather it makes God as vulnerable as we are, part of the same struggle, facing and enduring the same painful realities. He is on our side in the sense that he is with us in the same boat.

But how can that be? The second idea punctures a hole in traditional teaching about God's omniscience: that he knows everything about everything even before it happens. The future is as clear to him as the past so that right from the beginning his plan for our salvation, involving the death of Jesus, was all laid out. But a different way of thinking asks what it means to be creative and for God to be the great Creator? Intrinsic to creativity is not-knowing rather than knowing. By definition something new and unknown is lovingly brought into being - in God's case initially out of nothing whilst in our case out of what is to hand. The consequences of doing so may be predicted but cannot be known for certain. They may turn out as expected, or surprise and delight us beyond all expectation, or fill us with alarm and dismay like the alarming side effects of a new drug intended to heal. God's creativity is no different in that respect from ours. Creating cannot be an entirely safe enterprise. By definition it does not deal with the familiar but sails into uncharted waters.

So, to take the big example, God creates human beings in his image, giving them freedom and a creative potential similar to his own. Whilst the outcome was not without its pleasures it proved disastrous beyond all expectations. Men and women fell upon each other in ever more complex rounds of egocentric hostility, poisoning their personal relations and leading to growing conflict and injustice until Eden looked more like a bear garden. What was done could not be undone however - a sober reality which the story of Noah and God's attempt to start all over again only underlines. God's creative love now finds itself in much the same position as the creative love which remains in us despite the dark and destructive side of our personalities. It is a matter of being deeply involved in the struggle to overcome the consequences of what turned out to be a fateful decision.

This brings us to a third idea, and it runs contrary to traditional attempts to explain why Jesus died and what happened on the cross. Rather than the cost of sin, the cross has more to do with the cost of love. The life, death and resurrection of Jesus is not so much a story of what happened once upon a time when God sent his Son to die so that, justice being done, our sins could be forgiven. It is not a once-for-all event. The life, death and resurrection of Jesus represent the paradigm case, or supreme example, of what is happening all the time. God is always incarnate. God is always with us in the fray, continually acting out of creative love to resolve and heal and turn to good the terrible consequences of our misuses of the opportunities we were given. The Gospel stories of how he sides with outsiders, makes merry with the sad, has little of his own, champions the poor and despised, challenges power and deflates self-righteousness are insights into what such love means in practice. And the emerging and growing hostility are insights into what such love inevitably costs. The struggle to get humanity back on track requires a committed love which costs not less than everything.

The Cross of Calvary where Jesus is crucified between two thieves is replicated as it were in the gallows of the concentration camp where God is hanged by the neck between child and adult victims of the Holocaust. This is not what God planned. This was the unexpectedly expensive outcome of God's creative move. He is the victim along with us, helpless to undo what has been done but forever committed in costly love to make it good and get it back on a creative track, as Christ the Paradigm (different from us in degree but not in kind) makes clear.

One further idea reworks the traditional belief about God's omnipotence. So far we have built a picture of a good and loving God but, in the end, of a weak one who appears to have lost control. Having given it away, God now struggles to get a grip on things and in the meantime begins to look like a loser. The following `parable` (from Vanstone) however has helped me to think again. In it God is likened to a sculptor busy creating, say, a beautiful facial image. To some extent he can predict the effect of the next indentation he will make with his chisel. To some extent he cannot, and even less so if he has never attempted this kind of image before. At some point the chisel meets the stone and it is not long before the artist realises that he has made a false, not to say a disastrous, move. The image is defaced rather than enhanced. It is distressingly ugly rather than increasingly attractive, and what is done cannot be undone. But the power of the sculptor does not lie in his all-knowing ability to avoid false moves. His power and skill lie in his ability to continue to work with what he has now created until at the end of the day the outcome is even more attractive and satisfying than had that false move never been made. Costly love and creative ability combine to eventually make all things new. Dead ends come eventually to life.

Such an account of Christian faith goes a long way towards dealing with some of the issues we have raised. It offers us a way of understanding God's providential presence in our lives and reconciles the apparent contradiction between God's power and God's love. It doesn't ask us to believe in a once-for-all decisive event but an event which typifies what happens in history every day as God struggles with us to create a world. It doesn't claim a victory which we then find hard to see but corresponds with the long, long story of a world which moves forwards and backwards rather than forwards all the time and which seems all too difficult to transform into a peaceful and stimulating home for humanity. It even suggests a way of believing in resurrection by affirming the life-giving power of love, and of being more confident that at the end of the day, despite the set backs, God could achieve the new world of his dreams. It is a moving story of `Love's Endeavour, Love's Expense` (the title of one of Vanstone's books) within which we can set our lives and in which, as the friends of this Christlike God, we are invited to co-operate. And, as a story, it is compatible with a good deal of our experience. In other words, it fits!

But I cannot in the end say I find it wholly convincing. It deals with many of the problems we have discussed but by no means all of them. Whilst compatible with a good deal of our experience, it falls foul of the objection that some beliefs are so immune to the facts that they cannot be proved, or at least tested, one way or the other. Its idea of God is so different from what we usually mean by that term that it is in danger of adding very little to our appreciation of a historical process where certain kinds of well-intentioned activity turn out to be constructive and others do not, so that the God factor in the story becomes redundant. If it eschews ideas of historical progress in favour of fragmentary achievements, it is over-confident that in the end all will be well; and it assumes the existence of that other world which I find so hard to conceive.

Is any and every form of religious faith then doomed to be unsatisfactory and the whole idea of it therefore undermined? My answer to the first question is a definite `Yes` and to the second a tentative `No`.

III Man Made Faith

1. One insight more than any other has helped me to come to terms with the problems that surround my faith. It is not at all new, but when I took it to heart it proved its worth. It recognises that faith is a human construct or, to put it less formally, it accepts the humanity of religion including the humanity of its beliefs.

All our beliefs, whether we accept them or find them difficult to accept, are `man- made` or shall we say: `made by us`, to avoid sexist language. The biblical writings, which for many are their surest guide to Christian belief, are made by us or human beings like us: the work of many different authors, from prophets and psalmists to apostles and evangelists, over centuries. The creeds of the church, like the Apostles` Creed which many say every Sunday, and the Nicene Creed, are made by us. The hymns that we sing, for John Wesley the creed in song, are made by us. The doctrines of the church, such as the doctrines of Creation (that God made the world) and Atonement (that God through Christ redeemed it when things went badly wrong), together with all theological systems old and new, from the most traditional and orthodox to the most radical and revolutionary, are made by us, as are all the more personal stories we tell about the meaning of our lives.

Even claims which apparently run clean contrary to this idea and deny the humanity of religion, are made by us. Take the claim that the Bible is the revealed word of God. This can of course be quite a sophisticated claim. It does not necessarily imply that every word of it was dictated by God, or that it is entirely free from error, or that there are no human elements in the Bible. It does claim however that the Bible contains reliable information necessary for our salvation about God's ways with men and women and that that information comes to us, admittedly through human mediation, from God. It is not made by us; it is revealed. It is not mundane but divine. The point here however is that even this insistence or belief that biblical truth is God-given is itself made by us. In the end all our beliefs can be pushed back to this basic reality. Such beliefs would not and could not exist unless we human beings had made them up. Claims that Jesus is the incarnate Son of God, that he died for us upon the cross and that he rose again victorious over sin and death are all to be understood in the same way. So is the idea that we come to these conclusions not off our own bat but under the guidance of the Holy Spirit. The prophets and evangelists for example were obviously human beings but, whilst God was not holding the pen for them when they wrote, they were, it is claimed, inspired by God. So were the great teachers, doctors and leaders of the church and even the church itself. None of them achieved what they did on their own. They did not gain their insights unassisted. This was the work of the Holy Spirit. But such a belief in divine guidance and inspiration, alternately modest and audacious, is as `man-made` as all the rest.

Several factors understandably obscure the human nature of our beliefs and encourage us to set them apart from ideas which are more obviously our own. One is that so often they deal with subjects that are anything but human such as God, Jesus Christ, the Spirit, our salvation and eternal hope. Another is the fact that, if human beings made them up, those human beings did not include us. They have been handed down to us by the church over a long period of time stretching back through the centuries, so that by the time we received them, often in our childhood, they had taken on a very solid existence of their own. Or again, we have not exactly been encouraged to think of our beliefs in this rather down-to-earth way. The church has rarely if ever suggested to us that its teachings have feet of clay. Rather they have been entrusted to the church by God, tested and defended against the false ideas (heresies) of what were regarded as misguided - and often wicked - men and women, and handed on to us with all the faithfulness and authority the church can muster. But despite their divine subject matter, their longevity, their distance from us and the assurances of those who pass them on from one generation to another, they are `human constructs` (constructed or made by humans) nevertheless.

46

There are however important qualifications to be made. First of all, to insist that all our beliefs are made by us is not the same as suggesting that they are merely `made-up` in much the same way as a child might be accused of making up a story. In other words, if our beliefs are made by us, they are not mere fabrications or ideas conjured up out of thin air. We don't create them out of nothing! They are not simply lies or fantasies! They are reactions, more often than not thoughtful and genuine reactions, to something `there` either outside or inside of us or both. There are `givens` which are certainly not of our making. What is `there` may come close to a set of verifiable, historical facts: for example, a man called Jesus lived, taught, healed and died and attracted a great deal of admiring and hostile attention. Equally we could be talking about an unquestionable experience of great release and contentment, or of sudden illumination, or of change or healing. There is no suggestion that such things do not happen. But any attempt to describe what happened and to understand its significance - to make something of it shall we say - whether it be an incarnation or a miracle or a Damascus Road conversion, is made by us. Nobody makes up bird sounds, or a mountain covered with heather, or a running river, but the conclusion that `all things bright and beautiful` are made by God and are part of a good creation designed to delight us and win our praise and thanksgiving is made up by men and women like us.

To come to a second qualification, to insist that all religious beliefs are made by us is by no means to dismiss them as untrue. The Christian doctrine of Creation is made by us but that does not automatically mean that there is no God or that God did not make the heavens and the earth. Likewise with the church's beliefs in the divinity of Jesus and his victory over sin and death through his passion and resurrection: to humanise them is not to automatically falsify what they have to say. All scientific theories are human constructs and in their case we readily appreciate that they are not necessarily falsified by their human nature. The same can be said when I believe, for example, that my life is in the hands of a good God, or that it will not come to an end when I die and that in the hereafter I shall be dealt with justly and with mercy. The truth of our beliefs is not settled one way or another by their humanity, anymore than their human character pre-empts our earlier struggles (in chapter II) to make the claims of faith `fit` our experience.

What difference then does this insight make?   Once we accept the humanity of our beliefs we have to accept the human characteristics that go with it: characteristics that religious beliefs share with the people who made them, and treat those beliefs accordingly. Here are three of them.

2. First, our human limitations. We have many of course, including limits to our abilities and skills, but here we are talking about the limits to our knowledge and experience of the raw material out of which our beliefs are made.

Some beliefs arise out of quite specific and in some senses readily accessible areas of knowledge and experience such as ourselves or our human nature. The subject matter is not far away but on our doorstep. Even here however, despite the probing of psychology, sociology, medical science, biology, introspection and other relevant disciplines, we are far from knowing everything and a great deal remains a mystery. Quite a lot of believing has been built on what we claim to know about ourselves. Theologians often talk for example about the Nature of Man and Natural Theology or refer to Natural Law. Arguments about `nature` and `nurture`, or what is `natural`, or about the rights and wrongs of homosexuality or about the `selfish gene` and our ingrained perversity, all reflect links between what we know about ourselves and what as Christians we believe. But clearly our knowledge and understanding about what goes on inside us are limited and these limitations are illustrated by the way in which, as knowledge and experience grow, opinions can shift and beliefs change. What were regarded as the `natural`, God-given roles of women in society and the church, for example, are now called into question.

Some beliefs arise out of historical knowledge. They are responses to what happened in the past, often the very distant past. The key Christian events for example took place over 2000 years ago, whilst the history of the Jewish people, which provides the all-important background to those key events, goes back at least 2000 years before that. Christian faith originally sprang up in close proximity to those events when believers could have said with some justification: `we know, we were there`. Since then those early beliefs, whatever they were originally, have been elaborated over time in quite complex and sometimes contradictory ways within the varied traditions of Christianity. When we try to get back to the starting point to see what happened in the first place and what Christians originally made of it or what we might make of it now, we are quickly reminded of the limits to historical research (and therefore knowledge) despite the growing skills of the researchers. The evidence can be sparse. The documentation is never as complete as we would like and what there is is often written with attitudes to accuracy and historicity which were very different to ours.

Some of our beliefs are neither limited to particular areas of interest, like our beliefs about human nature, nor are they reactions to historical events. They are far more audacious and apparently embrace and claim to know something about everything. They make claims about the origins of the universe, the purpose of its existence and what the final outcome of life on earth will be. They also make claims as to how life has been brought about and will come to its conclusion. The great Christian saga of Creation, Fall, Incarnation, Redemption, Second Coming, Heaven and Hell leaves nothing out of its sweep.

However impressive, these claims to know everything are, nevertheless, made up by men and women who know comparatively little. These days we are continually reminded of

49

how little we know about the unimaginable reaches of space that exist beyond our tiny planet and its relatively small galaxy. Even the most up-to-date telescope or space probe takes us but a fraction of the way. We are also reminded of how little we know of the seemingly limitless past and unforeseeable future of the universe. The black holes of space provide an arresting image for the huge holes in our knowledge. Of any other world beyond this one, supernatural or non-material, we have no knowledge at all apart from out-of-body experiences, our own longings, and the messages of those who claim to mediate between us and the spirits of the dead.

Our knowledge as individuals is very limited indeed. No-one talks of `polyglots` these days, only of `know-alls` in derisive tones. When we get together things improve because we can usefully make up for one another's ignorance. We can supplement each other's insights as we look at life from different angles and pool information, so that the sum of our knowledge, past and present, is far greater than its parts. But even when we put it all together two realities still stare us in the face. One is the impossibility of completely joined-up thinking or of knowing how to fit all the pieces of the jigsaw together so that, fully co-operating, we could somehow between us gain a completely comprehensive and coherent view of things. Knowing all things, we still could not handle them. That is an ability we human beings do not have. Knowledge overload takes over. Second, if we have any sensitivity at all, given the sum of our knowledge, we remain acutely aware of just how much still remains to be discovered. We may wish to claim that the rest is knowable in principle, given time and advances in science (so that for example it is not that God's existence or non-existence is unknowable, only that we don't know it yet) and not forever beyond our knowing, but for all practical purposes it seems fair to say that for the present and foreseeable future there is more that we don't know than that we do. What we see is outweighed by the mysteries or unknowns which envelop us.

If then our religious beliefs are made by us, they are made by women and men whose knowledge is extensive and growing but severely limited, and the claims they make on the basis of it will inevitably share in those limitations. To the implications of that we must return.

3. A second human characteristic of our religious beliefs is that they are conditional. Just as a promise might be made on certain conditions (`you shall marry the prince if your shoe fits`) so our beliefs are held under certain conditions and those beliefs, like the promise, will be affected if the conditions change. There are three fairly obvious examples which have to do with culture, experience and personality.

Experience is an easy one to illustrate. One of the most familiar reasons that people give for falling out with God and ceasing to believe is the experience of suffering and loss when it comes close to home. They lose a loved one through accident, cancer or sudden death. They themselves contract a debilitating or life-threatening illness. They ask: `why me?`. They sense a lack of care on the part of God and injustice in the arbitrary decisions God apparently makes, since the question: `why me?` often carries the implication: `I don't deserve this`. So they decide there isn't a God after all or, if there is, he is not to their liking and they don't respect him or believe in him any more. If their experiences had been different and life (and God) had treated them well - if the shoe had fitted rather than pinched - they probably still would.

Of course events can run in almost the opposite direction. A hitherto rather superficial and unthinking (or shall we say `happy-go-lucky`) person suddenly has an experience which stops him in his tracks. Perhaps he is on holiday in an Asian or Africa country where he finds himself off the beaten track of the tourist trail and face to face with a degree of poverty and destitution he has never seen before. It stops him in his own tracks. He is shocked and disturbed. He starts to wonder what he is doing with his life and whether, if he goes on in the same old ways, it will ever add up to much. His experience leads to quite a turn-around, even to a sense of vocation. He now feels called to do some good whilst there is time and, beyond that, he is drawn to believe that the God he had previously dismissed as irrelevant has now come into his life in a quite decisive way.

To take a rather different example, a child grows up in a highly religious but not oppressive atmosphere. She experiences church going from an early age and regards it as a normal and natural part of her life. She likes and admires her parents as people who care not only for her but for all sorts of others like neighbours and friends, and who give generously to good causes. Although they have their faults and failings and she quarrels with them from time to time, she never feels that the gap between what they say they stand for and what they do is as wide and unacknowledged as to be hypocritical. She is never converted to faith as a born-again believer since she has believed from the start and nothing in her experience has suggested she should do otherwise.

A second child on the other hand grows up in a home where religion is hardly mentioned, except to cast doubt on it, and certainly never practised. It never occurs to anyone to go to church. The child however likes and admires her parents as people who care for her and others and actively support all sorts of worthwhile community activities. They have their faults and failings like the rest but there is something genuine, honest and straightforward about them which she admires. She has never really thought about believing in God and nothing in her experience to date suggests that she should.

We could write similar stories about people who hear voices and people who don't, or who escape terrifying storms and floods, or who encounter wonderful people, or recover from serious illness, or who are moved by the majesty of mountains, or feel new energies stirring inside them. The point is that we haven't all had the same experiences and one of the reasons why we don't all believe the same things has to do with the experiences we have had or have not had and the impact they did or did not make on us.

To take a second example, beliefs are also culturally conditioned, a point we touched on earlier when we noted how aspects of Christian belief, like miracles, visions and prophesies which seem incredible to the Western secular-minded among us, are often perfectly believable to Christian communities in the South. They are far from ignorant of Western intellectual ideas but are not so totally dominated by them and the biblical world seems more familiar and closer to their own.

If you live in a God-accepting culture you are more likely to believe than if you don't. A small-scale, but important example of this is churchgoing. People will say that they go to church or to the mosque because they believe; but the reverse is equally true, if not more so: they believe because they go to church or the mosque and are continually confirmed by what is said and done there in the faith system that runs through it all. They may stop going because something has happened in their lives to undermine their faith; but equally if they stop going they may well find that their faith begins to fall away rather rapidly and is increasingly difficult to recover without returning.

For me, the most memorable examples of the difference made by culture were my visits to friends in India. At home in England and infected by secularisation I could often be acutely embarrassed by being regarded as a religious person, and uncomfortable with practices like family prayers and grace at meals (other than Quaker-type silences which simply provide opportunities to feel grateful rather than give thanks to God!). In India, staying with what in England would have been regarded as a very pious couple, I felt quite differently as we read the Bible, said morning prayers together in the home and prayed, sometimes at length, before every meal. God, the holy, and religious faith (Christian or otherwise) were part of the ordinariness of life in a way, at home in the West, they were

53

not. Religion was intrinsic to the culture and I felt more at ease to be part of it.

A rather heady mixture of these `conditions`, including our experiences, our cultural surroundings and what we might call accidents of geography and history (when and where we were born and live for example), have an enormous influence on whether we are religious believers or not and, if we are, on what kind of beliefs we hold: Christian, Baptist, Anglican, Orthodox, Muslim, Sikh, Hindu or whatever. One set of circumstances can take us in one direction and another in the opposite.

A third example of the way in which faith is conditioned has to do with our personalities. For reasons we may never understand there are people for whom the glass is always half-full whilst for others it is always half-empty. The former may be more inclined to take a hopeful view of life and faith than the latter. Again, some people are by nature more reflective and sceptical than others and more likely to have difficulties with believing instead of taking much of it for granted There are the confident types, at home in their own skin and at ease with the world, and there are those who, shy and nervy, find all too many situations a threat. Unsure of themselves and everyone else they may well be glad to have a personal, ever-present Father God to rely on. Personality can influence the kind of beliefs we adopt and whether we believe at all.

The argument here is that once we understand the humanity of our beliefs we have to accept that, like all things human, they are conditioned. They are `manufactured` or made up under certain conditions and had those conditions been different, faith would have been different too. There is an interesting, large-scale historical example of this from the fourth century and the time when the seat of empire moved from Rome to Constantinople. The move left a political vacuum in Rome which the church there soon filled to become a powerful political presence. The church in the East (Orthodox) on the other hand, living close to the imperial power, became far more subservient and `obedient to the powers appointed by God`. Institutional Christian obedience took on a distinctive flavour in both camps which might well have been different in both cases had conditions been otherwise.

But, to be clear, if faith is conditioned by our experiences, by culture, by historical events and accidents, and by our personalities, it is not determined by them. Suffering and untimely death may come into a person's life and lead to a loss of faith in God. It could and does however often leave that faith undisturbed or even deepened. Instead of asking: `Why me? `, some will ask: `Why not me? `, and be content to trust God and God's mysterious but, they are quite sure, ultimately benevolent ways. The child of a kindly, church-going family may in the end reject the faith of his fathers rather than continue in it as the `natural` thing to do. Indeed offspring of the same parents may well move in opposite directions, one towards faith and another away from it. Confronted by the realities of poverty in the world it is still possible to shrug them off, or to see only the absence of God in them rather than discerning his presence, or to respond to them thoughtfully but without any reference to religious beliefs. Miraculous escapes from storms or diseases, or the spectacle of beautiful sunsets do not automatically turn everyone towards God. There are plenty of religious believers in the West, despite its secularised culture, and plenty of secularists in India. And if our personalities give us a disposition to move in certain directions it does not always mean we do so. We may `act out of character` as they say.

Of course the explanations for these unexpected outcomes may lie deeper in a great many more conditioning factors which we need to take into account. It is likely, for example, that the child of pious parents who in the end rejects their faith will have had a different set of experiences in adult life from the one who continues to share it. Circumstances and culture as well as personality may well affect one's reaction to a sunset. One traveller may be more open than another to the moral impact of poverty as a result of unsettling events which occurred before she ever set out. It might very well be that our beliefs and actions are wholly conditioned but that we do not as yet have a complete picture of what those complex conditioning factors are and how they interact with one another.

Here we come across a long-running (philosophical and theological) debate which can be seen as a battle between two `faiths` since there is, at present, no conclusive proof either way (only perhaps what common sense might suggest). On one side are those who believe that our lives are wholly determined. On the other side are those who hold very strongly to the view that we have the freedom to choose, even the God-given freedom. We do not have to resolve this dispute however, even if we could, or take sides to make our point. Whether wholly or in part, the conditions under which we construct and maintain our faith affect what that faith will be like. Under different conditions we would undoubtedly believe otherwise.

4. We turn to a third human characteristic of our beliefs. They are not only held with a large degree of ignorance and affected by changeable conditions, they are also self-interested. To suggest that a good deal of what we believe, like most things we do, is marked by self-interest may sound like a bald statement which comes nearer to an article of faith than a factual observation. The accusation certainly features prominently in the Christian tradition where sin, and with it self-centredness, play a major role in its understanding of human nature (or `doctrine of man`). If disobedience to God comes first on the list of heinous crimes, lack of love for our neighbour runs a close second. But let me rehearse three familiar points before we go further.

First, if self-interest is an important factor in our behaviour it is not, on the surface at least, the only one. Over and over again people put others before themselves and their own interests. They care for others; they give up their time to voluntary work; they go without for the sake of their children; they put themselves at risk to protect or stand by someone else; they give to charity; they die heroically in battle; they donate for medical purposes; they suffer for the sake of justice even to the point of martyrdom. Of course we can argue that self-interest is at work even here. Generous actions like these bring us self-satisfaction. Other people will think better of us. If we acted otherwise we could not live with ourselves. It's a pleasure, or only natural, to sacrifice for our children. Outgoing behaviour brings its own rewards. All that is true, and it is important to be aware of how deep self-interest can go, but that does not mean that all human behaviour is equally unpleasant and unhelpful where the only person who seems to matter or is ever considered is `me`.

Second, self-interest is not an entirely bad thing. Take the phrase: `love your neighbour as yourself` or the golden rule: `do to others as you would wish them to do to you`. They seem to strike a healthy balance whereas, for example, self-hatred strikes us as distinctly unhealthy and often destructive. Again, a measure of self-interest and looking after number one can add up to the kind of responsibility which ensures that we are not an unnecessary burden on other people. It could even be said that we have a duty to take care of ourselves. To go even further, a measure of self-love, far from being the antipathy to the kind of self-forgetfulness that loves and cares for others, may actually reflect that degree of personal security which provides exactly the right springboard from which to reach out to them.

Third, self-interest, where it does become destructive rather than healthy, is not necessarily a `sin` or a moral failing. In the Christian tradition selfish, destructive behaviour has all too often been seen as the offspring of our fundamental disobedience to God. It breaks the rules which God has drawn up to moderate our relations with one another and with him. Broken and ignored they lead to disrupted, unhappy and conflictual relationships rather than good ones. The way to deal with them is for us on our part to realise what we are doing and change our ways: in other words to repent, and for the wronged party, including God, to forgive.

Self-interested behaviour however is not so much born of sinful disobedience to rules, as of insecurity. Once again we must be aware of a long-running argument which we cannot resolve and do not need to. We can be heard to say that bad and selfish behaviour is always the result of unfortunate experiences, like being insecure in childhood, or unloved, or rejected or whatever, and is never our fault. We are automatons. Our behaviour is simply the result of what other people do to us and the buttons they happen to press. It might be true except that not everyone apparently reacts to bad experiences in the same negative and predictable ways and, in any case, if we treat people as having no mind or will of their own we shall soon treat them in highly patronising, controlling and disrespectful ways, and not like human beings.

That having been said, insecurity is an indelible mark of the human condition at all kinds of levels. We can be insecure within ourselves, insecure about our relationships, fearful of losing trust and love, insecure in terms of livelihoods and money, insecure about our reputations and jobs, insecure in the obvious sense of possible dangers against which we lock the door, set the alarm, and try to defend ourselves, insecure about the future and that of future generations. Our hold on life is fragile. Illness, accident and death can rob us of it at any moment. We are mortal. Over and above all this our lives are, as it were, surrounded by uncertainty. Unless we have opted for the certainties of divine revelations and are completely convinced by them, we do not know how we got here, for what purpose if any we are alive on this earth, where we are going, or anything much about the vast mysteries that surround us: endless physical space and endless intellectual puzzles and endless spiritual heights and depths. That is why we are so busy with our human constructs, trying to get a handle on the unknown, naming and taming and making some sense of it all.

Being insecure, our natural instinct, rather than our sinful determination, is to do whatever we can to protect ourselves and make ourselves safe. Our behaviour becomes egocentric. We look after number one. Given the choice, we take the decision which, as far as we can tell, is most likely to benefit us: to increase our standing, improve our financial prospects, maintain our health, ingratiate us with others, keep the enemy at bay and the wolf from the door, help us to hold on to what we've got. In our insecurity we watch out for ourselves and that is usually, if not always, to the detriment of others.

So self-interest, with all its negative results, is not necessarily a sign of perversity but, due to our insecurity, it does pervade our lives, including our beliefs. We tend to favour the beliefs that, in our judgment, will benefit ourselves. Let me take a small-scale and a large-scale example.

In the New Testament there are subtle differences between the Gospels and how they report the sayings of Jesus. In Luke 6.20 Jesus apparently says: `Blessed are the poor for theirs is the Kingdom of God`. We can readily understand that saying to mean that in the long run those without money food or shelter, the `have-nots` marginalised by the `haves`, will come out on top. Their day will finally dawn, and it might be better to be among them! In Matthew 5.3 however Jesus apparently says: `Blessed are the poor in spirit` which can just as readily be understood to mean that what matters is not whether you are rich or poor in a material sense but in a spiritual sense. It's your attitude that matters, for example, and whether you are humble and reliant on God, not your bank balance. We do not know of course why any change took place, if indeed it did, or whether we have correctly interpreted the difference between the two, but we can easily imagine, in the world we know, which of them might be preferred by those who are relatively comfortably off and, with enough to be anxious about, want to hang on to what they've got. We can also guess which interpretation might appeal to those who've had a raw deal. You believe according to your interests.

On a much larger scale we might make a crude comparison between two different types of Christianity. One we will call `privatised`. It is concerned about the private relationship between the individual and God. The relationship has come to grief, in traditional teaching because of our disobedience, and steps have been taken to put matters right. If we have faith in the redeeming work of God in Jesus then we can be forgiven and our relationship with God restored. But it is essentially a private matter and equally relevant to rich and poor alike since all have sinned and come short of the glory of God. This change in our relationship with God certainly leads us to change our behaviour but the changes again have to do with rather private and personal matters like sex and whether we are kind and charitable towards our neighbours. The change has much less, if anything, to do with upheavals in the social, economic or political orders, certainly not directly. (This form of religion was reflected, for whatever reasons, in `A Short Guide to the Duties of Church Membership`, issued by the Archbishops of Canterbury and York, published by SPCK, where much was said about personal devotion, family life and service to the church but little if anything about public affairs beyond personal service to the community.)

Such a private religion in its purest form my well be a `straw man`, especially if we set out to castigate it rather than understand it. We can easily think, for example, of people and traditions which have believed very strongly that this is the heart of Christianity and that until matters are put right between me and God nothing else of much good can follow. But at times, such Christians (`evangelicals` amongst them) have also been at the forefront of radical social movements: to abolish slavery for example or, in more recent times, the debts of poor countries. Again there may be good and understandable reasons (to which we shall return in chapter IV) for a more `private` religion. In the Western world there came a time when the church was seen to be far too powerful and dictatorial, ruling the roost in every walk of life from personal morals to political affairs. Reducing the sphere of religion from the public to the private realm was a way of cutting that church down to size.

It is possible however to conceive of other factors at work when we keep religion in its place and regard it only as a private affair. If you are in a position of power for example and the present order of things is to your advantage, you will much prefer a set of Christian (or any other religious) beliefs that tends to keep things more or less as they are and does not disturb the status quo. And if it actually helps or encourages the less well off to put up with things, because what really matters in the long run is their standing with God, or because if they remain faithful in this life they will be rewarded in the next, or even because rulers are appointed by God and other than obeying them they are not our concern, then so much the better. Privatised religion, promoted by powerful people, can be seen to be in their self-interest. Marx, with his critique of religion as the opiate of the people, could be heard to criticise it very much along these lines.

A quite different type of Christianity has, since the latter part of the 20th Century, been associated with Liberation Theology. Far from religion being a private matter between the individual and God it is now a very public matter. Far from the essential problem being a broken personal relationship and slavery to sin, the problem is a pernicious and oppressive social order that enslaves vast numbers of people in poverty and servitude. Far from a personal relationship that needs putting right it is the social order that needs revolutionising so that the poor, and the rich for that matter, are liberated from it. Far from the Gospel applying equally to everyone because all have sinned, it makes the poor and their plight a priority, not to mention God's priority. Far from social change and politics being on the edge of a Christian's concerns they are right at the centre. The essence of Christianity is better caught by a new Moses leading slaves in a new Exodus, or by the Magnificat where the mighty are brought down from their thrones and the poor are lifted high, or by the great reversals signalled by Jesus in his teaching where the last become first and the least the greatest and the outsider comes in from the cold to take centre stage. And it is the threat of such disturbances that may well have persuaded the rulers of his day to do away with him.

As we have already seen, a concern for an individual's right relations with God and a concern for just relations within society are not incompatible. They can even be complementary. One is clear that societies won't change unless the people who make them up change. The other is clear that people are more than individuals and are often prevented from changing by the social conditions under which they live. There may well be truth in both.

Once again however it is possible to see how this more public and `revolutionary` form of Christian believing can be attractive to certain groups of people because they perceive it to be in their self-interest. This time it is not of course the rich and powerful, who would much prefer to keep the status quo, but the underdogs who have little to lose and much to gain from radical change. Liberation Theology has by no means only flourished among the poor but, not surprisingly, it has often found its warmest welcome there.

Just as it was easy to think of examples where people don't necessarily act selfishly so it is easy to think of religious beliefs which don't appear to be self-interested. Once again however they may be reminders of just how subtle self-interest, not necessarily a bad thing in itself, can be and how deep it can go. The ultimate, selfless sacrifice of forsaking everything to follow Jesus (or Mohammed) may nevertheless carry its own attractive rewards. Whoever loses their life for my sake will find it. Vivid descriptions of an after-life, full of retribution and threats of divine punishments for our misbehaviour and lack of faith, make for very uncomfortable reading. Self-interest may lead some to re-interpret them or `explain them away` as having more to do with the God of the Old Testament for example than the Christlike God of the new. Self-interest may on the other hand lead some to hold on to them as one element in a stick and carrot approach to themselves and to others. Certainly in the past the fear of Hell has been used by many a preacher to instil the fear of God into their congregations `for their own good` as well as by authority figures to instil respect and compliance in those they seek to control.

Religion then, whilst dealing with the divine, is essentially human, characterised by human limitations, conditioned by personality, experience and circumstance, and shot through with self-interest. Seeing it clearly in this way, what difference does it make?

IV Treating Religion as Human

In the previous chapter we recognised the fact that religious faith is a human construct. Our beliefs are made by us or `man-made`, even those which claim they are revealed and God-given and seem to deny their essential humanity. This does not mean that they are necessarily untrue or conjured up out of thin air, but it does mean that they inevitably share our human characteristics. They share the limitations of our knowledge. They are conditioned as we are by experience, culture and personality; and they are shot through with self-interest. What are the implications of all this?

I. The most obvious implication seems to be the very opposite of what we might look to religion to provide. We are left drifting about without an anchor in a sea of uncertainty. We may have felt sure about God's love and our salvation and destiny, but we can no longer be sure since, had circumstances been different, we might have felt equally sure about something else. We are forced to come to terms with what is often referred to as `relativism`.

Relativism acknowledges exactly the points we have been making: that our beliefs are `relative`. They depend on their relationship with something else like the extent of our knowledge or our current pre-occupations: if those change then our beliefs are likely to change with them. Our beliefs are not wholly independent and impervious to their surroundings. Even more unsettling conclusions can follow. Since all our beliefs are affected in this way: since all are relative and the children of changing circumstances, there is nothing to choose between them. In the end one is as good as another or, more accurately, one is no better than all the others. Anything goes and nothing goes. None shall have prizes because none has won.

Whilst there may be truth in that, as we shall see, it can also be a slight on the relativist's position. To say that every religious belief is relative is not necessarily to say that every belief should be treated with equal respect. There are ways of sorting them out. One we have already discussed at some length when we talked about

64

`Making Faith Fit`. Some beliefs fit with the facts of life, or how we experience it, better than others. Where they don't, they frequently go through the refiner's fire and may even get discarded. But that is not the only test.

Another has to do with the longevity of a belief and how widespread it has become. That is not because the older a belief is the better, and the more who believe it the merrier, as if age and statistics were everything. Rather, if it has been exposed to many different people at many different times and in many different places, so bringing to it a wide variety of experiences, cultures and points of view; if it has been tried and tested in this way, then it has a better claim to be taken seriously than, say, the novel idea of an isolated sect. That is but one reason for studying a tradition like the Christian tradition with great care.

Again, beliefs can be opened up to debate about their internal logic and reasoning. Do they make sense or are they nonsense or even self-contradictory? Some of the long-running debates in Christianity about articles of faith that have come to look like revealed truths are in fact debates about just that. The high-sounding doctrine of the Trinity for example emerges painfully from efforts to avoid Christian self-contradiction and reconcile the belief in a Father God, God the Son, and God the Holy Spirit with the much older commitment to monotheism or belief in only one God. Again it has not been easy to hold together the belief in Christ's divinity and his humanity, or the fact that in Jesus the God who does not change and is `impassible` (incapable of suffering) suffered the pains of human beings.

A rather different way of choosing between different, relative beliefs is to turn on its head one of the factors that contributes to that relativity. Because human self-interest is everywhere, all beliefs must be subject to what is referred to in the scholarly world as `the hermeneutics of suspicion`. Hermeneutics is the business of understanding and explaining texts and ideas. `What exactly is it

65

saying?' To do so with 'suspicion' is to acknowledge that a belief, like a text, will not be properly understood unless you ask who is saying and believing it and why and, in this case, with what vested interests (which need not necessarily be malign) in mind. You need to know where the believer is coming from to understand the real force of his or her faith. You don't simply take things at their face value. Many a white South African Christian in the past believed that God wanted black and white people to develop separately and they interpreted the Bible, especially parts of the Old Testament, as backing up that conviction. To realise that those Christian believers came from a minority group with an interest in hanging on to its wealth and power was to understand a great deal, maybe everything, about the nature of their belief in apartheid. We made similar comments about the interest of the powerful in a private version of faith which is unlikely to disturb the status quo, and the interest of the poor in a faith which most likely will. Religion as a 'comfort zone' also raises questions about the interests, often understandable, of those who cling to it.

We can however turn this somewhat negative factor on its head and choose between different beliefs on the basis of which of them, if held, seems most likely to benefit the most people or, as it is sometimes put, serve the common good. A belief in the equal importance of all women and men in the sight of God seems far more promising on that basis than notions of God-given racial superiority, or gender or hierarchical authority and deference. To put it in another way, beliefs which promote the self-interest of the many may well be preferable (if not always preferred in practice!) to those which serve only the interests of a few.

Relativism then does not necessarily mean that there is nothing to choose between one relative belief and another. There may however be no way of finalising the debate. For one thing we can throw doubts on all the criteria we have just mentioned. Facts are slippery things and can be undermined by so-called new facts. A broad catholic consensus could still be wrong. Majorities are no guarantee of what is true or what is right. What almost everybody believed to be in their self-interest (subduing the earth to produce economic growth for example) could still turn out not to be the case (if it threatens sustainability and happiness and contributes to global warming). The consequences of believing something are rather hard to predict or even trace with hindsight.

More seriously still, in trying to weigh up the merits of our beliefs there is no final arbiter to which we can turn which is itself free from the very relativity from which we may be trying to escape: no book, no creed, no institution, no charismatic teacher, no authority, even though, as we have said, some may be more worthy of our attention than others. There are then ways of choosing between beliefs and the arbiters of beliefs, but there may be no way of finally coming to rest. What then are we to do?

Accepting the humanity of our religion we have to embrace our own humanity in two respects. The first we have not so far mentioned, and that is the need for us to shoulder the responsibility of deciding for ourselves what we're going to believe. That does not mean deciding by ourselves. For one thing we can't, since we are not alone in this world and, like it or not, we are surrounded and influenced (conditioned) by all sorts of people and experiences. Almost all of us for example are born into a faith tradition of one kind or another that will inevitably affect our thinking. For another thing, it would be foolish to come to decisions on our own and ignore all the knowledge and insights to hand which, if considered carefully, can help us to decide more wisely. Again, deciding for ourselves does not mean that we can decide between everything and anything. The range of opinions open to us is limited, often by those very same marks of our humanity. We don't, for example, know what all the options are even if we have read and travelled widely, and our personal fears, inclinations and interests inhibit us from going down certain routes. Some things we are ready to see whilst remaining blind to others. We may of course take a quite different option and hand over our responsibility for deciding what we believe to someone or something else: to a church, or book, or a person whose authority in these matters we have come to respect. Such an act of abdication, submission or trust is still however our decision, the responsibility for which remains ours.

Since all and everything is relative and none of the reasons for believing or not believing are final however impressive the evidence or the arguments, the ultimate answer to: `why do you believe in God? `, or the Resurrection of Jesus from the dead, or the coming of the Kingdom is `because I have decided to`. Some thinkers (existentialist philosophers for example) and to an extent our own common sense suggest that taking responsibility and being decisive in this way is a very important part of what it means to be human. Those who fail to do so can strike us as inadequate or immature. There is also a pragmatic reason as to why it is necessary to decide and that is because the alternative can be paralysis. We cannot co-operate with others for example without some decision as to how far we can rely on the apparent common ground between us, a decision which cannot finally rest on incontrovertible evidence. How far this is true of our religious beliefs is not so clear. We can be agnostic about many things and get on with life very well At times however life is going to grind to a halt if we forever wait for our minds to be made up for us or fail to make them up for ourselves.

The main point however is this: that what we believe finally rests on our own decisions, a point which is reflected in some rites of passage. For example, Christian infant baptism recognises the extent to which we don't choose the beliefs that will surround and influence us as we grow up. They are a parental and cultural gift, whilst confirmation (or for some Christians like Baptists, believers baptism), when we answer for ourselves, underlines that as we grow into responsibility, the choice to hold on to that gift is finally ours.

Once we accept the humanity of religion then we also have to embrace our own humanity and accept the need to make up our own minds, deciding what to believe and taking responsibility for it. This decisiveness however, which has to have a certain firmness and resilience about it so that it doesn't collapse so readily that it really isn't a decision at all, has to be married with what we might call a certain modesty, above all as to whether it was the right decision to make. As we have seen, it could have been made for questionable reasons. New information or fresh experiences may one day cast a different light on it. Made with undoubted sincerity and conviction it is still quite possibly mistaken. Believers are decisive but nevertheless modest about the claims they make for the veracity of their beliefs. They do and do not put them beyond question. Such a double-minded, almost schizophrenic, attitude is harder for some to achieve than others. To call it a sign of religious maturity, as I am tempted to do, may be unhelpful and even disrespectful to those who, on the one hand, feel that integrity in matters of religious belief only lies in not making up your mind at all and to those who, on the other hand, see their faith as either wholehearted and beyond question or nothing.

If we are to have religious faith however its humanity and ours seem to imply both the need for us to make up our minds and decide what that faith is to be, and the need to be modest about those very decisions. There is no more room for dogmatism here than there is in completely dismissing religious claims, since both are subject to the human characteristics, including our limited knowledge, which we have described.

If we want to talk in terms of `truth` (what philosophers sometimes refer to as `truth claims`), some arguments we have about what is true and what is not are more straightforward than others. We can sometimes produce the evidence to prove a point and that is that. When it comes to our religious beliefs however matters are not so straightforward.

We can test our beliefs, as we have said, in all sorts of ways: against reason, experience, the `facts` (a tricky word) as we think we know them, long tradition, writings and voices we have come to respect, people and events we are tempted to describe as `a revelation` to us, intuition, as well as against all those other human beings in our communities who fortunately don't always see things as we do. That kind of testing and the energetic conversations it involves could be described as a serious search for truth, so serious in fact that it can feel pretty conclusive. Our response however, for all the human reasons we have talked about, will stop short of saying: `It is the truth`. We may be convinced, but there are always questions to be raised, more to be discovered and other perspectives to be taken into account, so we know we cannot finally dig in our heels. I would not put it in this highly believing way, but I like the modesty and openness of the old hymn: `The Lord has yet more light and truth to break forth from his word! `

I turn now to look at the implications of the humanity of religion not generally but in more practical and particular ways.

2.   First of all what does it imply about our ethical values and moral rules: about what we regard as good and what we think we ought to do? They too can take on a very solid and permanent air and seem anything but `human constructs` or ideas we human beings have made up. They confront us with all their seemingly independent claims and demands. It certainly doesn't feel as though we construct them. In fact `making the rules up for yourself` or ` as you go along` seems to be the very opposite of what morality is about!

There are a number of reasons why they appear to be so solid. First they seem solid because we have traditionally thought of so many of them as God-given. The Ten Commandments, delivered from the mountain top on tablets of stone, are a classic example. The moral teaching embedded in the Quran would have a similar divine imprimatur. Second, moral rules seem solid because they are said to be rooted in the way things are or, as the moralist would say, they are part of `natural law`. A well-known example is the argument that because the very nature and purpose of sexual intercourse is to make babies it is wrong or `unnatural` to practice it, for example, with the use of condoms, when its purpose is deliberately denied or frustrated. An extension of that argument, recognising that babies are the offspring of relationships between men and women, leads to moral disapproval of sex outside of marriage. Similar arguments, based on what is `natural`, have been mounted against homosexuality. Morality has to do with the way things are whether we like them that way or not. A third reason why moral rules appear to be so solid is their longevity and universality: they seem to have been around for as long as we can remember and they are acknowledged, even if not acted upon, by everyone. Recently, as inter-faith dialogue has developed, there have even been attempts to distil a `global ethic` from the teachings of all the world's religions, suggesting that there are indeed rules and values which, despite our many differences, we all have in common. The Golden Rule, commanding us to treat others as we would wish them to treat us, or to love our neighbours as ourselves, is one of them.

There is nothing here however which ultimately denies that, despite appearances, moral rules and values are made by us. To say that the rules come from God is a `man-made` belief as we have seen, like all ideas about revelation. To say that moral rules are rooted in nature and the way things are is only to throw us back on the attempts we have made to understand the whys and wherefores of our world: what exactly is its nature?; static or evolving?; involving or resisting human interference?; and then to produce theories and theologies to capture our conclusions. And the longevity and universality of moral rules, however impressive and useful, does not alter the fact that human beings made them up a long, long time ago and, as time went by, most of those who followed simply came to similar conclusions.

Moral rules and values are as human as the religious beliefs with which they are often associated. Once again that does not mean they were simply fabricated for no good reason or that they are

71

untrue or not worthy of our respect but, as with our beliefs, it does mean that, being human, they share our human characteristics and should be treated accordingly. They too are subject to inevitable limitations so that new knowledge may call them into question; they too are conditioned by personality (note how quickly `what I like` begins to suggest what others should like as well), culture and circumstances; and they too can be shot through with self-interest. Like our beliefs they are relative.

Three different approaches to moral rules can help us to think about their relativity. One approach (technically called `deontological`) thinks of them in terms of duty (deontos). They tell us what we ought to do: we ought to do our duty whatever the consequences or circumstances. It is your duty to tell the truth even if it gets your best friend into trouble. It is your duty to be loyal and fight for your country even if it is engaged in a disastrous war. A second approach (technically called `teleological`) insists that the morality of an action depends on its aim or outcome. A good rule should produce good results. It is its `end` (telos) that matters. You should be faithful in marriage because that is best for the happiness and well-being of yourself, your partner, your children and society in general. You should always tell the truth because it fosters an atmosphere of trust. A third approach (technically called `situationist` or `contextual`) tends to say: `well it all depends`. In some situations it may be good to tell the truth but not in others especially if the result brings a whole lot more trouble and unhappiness than if you had told a white lie or said nothing. Again, where the unborn child is severely abnormal rather than mildly so, an unwavering respect for life in all its forms may, in this painful situation, have to give way to abortion.

There is a lot to discuss about these three approaches, how they interact with one another and the difficulties which each one of them raises. Arguments can become complex and tangled with not very clear cut results. Our present purpose however is only to underline just how full of IFS and BUTS they are even where the situationist approach is not being consciously adopted. A rule or act is `good` IF it produces a satisfactory outcome. In other words its goodness is relative to its effects or consequences. Telling a lie could then be morally justified IF all it did was to avoid hurting someone's feelings. BUT it would be less justified IF it respected their feelings at the cost of helping them to face reality. Doing your duty may at first sight appear to be above this kind of relativism BUT what IF two duties: to be loyal to your country for example and to act justly, clash with one another? Can we in practice find many examples of moral rules, beyond the very general and bland like loving your neighbour, about which we can honestly say they should be kept without any exception whatsoever: no IFS and BUTS?

If moral rules are relative in this way they are also characterised, like our beliefs, by self-interest. They tend to sound impartial and indeed a standard test of a moral rule is whether it can be applied equally or impartially to everyone. But, like laws, moral rules can be promulgated and promoted by those most likely to benefit if they are kept: by men as against women for example. It may well be our duty, following the advice of more than one New Testament text, to respect certain people and bow to authority figures and governing bodies, but we should be well aware of who is telling us to do so.

Once we accept the humanity of moral rules and values much the same arguments follow as in the case of our beliefs. Relative as they are it does not mean we cannot choose between them by testing them against their track record and their resilience to changing circumstances, by looking to see how widely they are held and respected and by trying to estimate the benefits they will bring. But once again in those often difficult discussions (over the rights and wrongs of homosexual relations for example) there is no final arbiter above the human fray to settle matters once and for all and we are left with much the same options as before. We can choose to hand over authority to someone or something else, like the Bible or the church, or we can take on the responsibility of deciding for ourselves. Once again that does not mean deciding by ourselves.

We shall draw on all the wisdom we can get from our faith communities and elsewhere. In the end however the responsibility is our own. One practical way of combining the two is to work for consensus whereby many insights are taken into account whilst, along with others, we accept personal ownership of the outcome.

The point about paralysis setting in if we fail to make up our minds is more telling in the case of moral rules and values. The relationship between them and our actions is often more immediate than between our actions and our religious beliefs. Of course we may not be the least interested in acting in a morally principled way (the strong streak of egoism born of insecurity which we have already discussed will make certain of that) but if and when we are, then a permanent indecisiveness over the right thing to do will freeze us in our tracks. Decisiveness however, important as it is, needs a more modest and less confident companion. Having put our hand to the moral plough, firmly committed to pacifism or opposed to abortion or whatever, there is a sense in which, contrary to the biblical injunction, we ought to look back or at least over our shoulders because we have not forgotten just how human those commitments are. Once again, being decisive is not the same as being dogmatic.

This sense that moral debates are never quite at an end and probably should not be, will become more acute the more we move from general rules, where there are few if any IFS and BUTS, to deciding about more particular cases. It is fairly easy to reach consensus on loving our neighbours or on respect for life and it is quite hard to imagine fundamental objections being raised. Things become much more difficult when it comes to asking what it means to love your neighbour, for example in a fraught debate about immigration, or what it means to respect life in matters of peace and war, or when faced with chronic or terminal illness. We still have to take decisions and act if we are to be of any use to anyone including ourselves but, acutely aware of their relativity and humanity, we shall keep a half-open mind about them. New knowledge, another perspective, changed circumstances, fresh disclosures of interest could make all the difference.

3. Looking at some practical implications of the humanity of religion we turn, secondly, to inter-faith relations. Here of course we may immediately confront the view that this whole way of understanding of religion is wrong (though we can just as easily confront it in our internal relations between Christians and fellow Christians). It can be dismissed by the ancient religious traditions of Asia for example, if not with total incomprehension then as far too Western and cerebral. It assesses the basis for religious belief too exclusively on an intellectual level and largely ignores the experiential. Or again Islam, as I understand it, will categorically deny any talk of a man-made religion, insisting that the Quran was literally dictated in Arabic by God and that Mohammed was neither more nor less than the faithful messenger of what God had said; and it will point to substantial internal evidence, including the style and beauty of the Quran, to prove it. The very premise of this discussion: that religion is a human construct, will be challenged in inter-faith dialogue and it would be a denial of all that has been said if we were not to open ourselves to that challenge.

Until our minds are changed however our sceptical approach to the nature of religious beliefs remains. These beliefs may well respond to realities in our experience as we try to make sense of them. Our conclusions, whether about God or salvation or the future, are not necessarily mistaken. They are nevertheless made by us and therefore share our human characteristics. As such they are not completely beyond dispute. As a result we shall take another set of religious beliefs as seriously as our own as equally serious efforts to get at the truth about our lives, but we shall also ask the same potentially undermining questions of them as we do of our own.

Any such questioning however will be subject to moral constraints. The overall aim will be constructive, balancing the differing claims of truth, of greater understanding, of peaceful co-existence, and of increasing co-operation and mutually beneficial relationships. Questions will only be asked and explored in appropriate circumstances such as in the privacy of our own reading and reflection, or in scholarly discussions, or in debates where the rules of engagement are well understood, or above all within growing relationships of trust where the sincerity and goodwill of all involved is acknowledged and accepted. There will need to be very good and urgent reasons for inaugurating anything like an aggressive or hostile interrogation so easily interpreted as lacking in respect.

Ideally what should gradually emerge are inter-faith encounters of complete mutuality. We hold our beliefs with conviction and so do they. Ours are human and open to question and so are theirs. Criticisms will be voiced since respecting someone else's religion, like respecting their culture, does not make it sacrosanct. But these encounters will be potentially far more constructive than that. One view may help to correct another. Beyond that it may complement if not complete it. For example Muslim insights into the central importance of `jihad` or spiritual struggle, if we are to win our salvation, may complement Christian emphases on salvation as a gift or by grace alone, and vice versa. Buddhist insights into the temporary nature of the ego or self, comprising strands of ongoing life which come together at birth and separate again after a while at death, may complement the Christian emphasis on the dignity of the individual and vice versa. Islam's opposition to Riba or lending money with excessive interest and without risk could be a healthy challenge to Western Christianity's connivance at usury and its embrace of capitalism. So we learn from one another and grow wiser together. We may even reach a fresh understanding of `conversion` where the aim is no longer for one `side` to persuade the other of the rightness of its claims (though there is no reason why people should not be so persuaded) and to join it, but for both to move beyond (or be converted out of) their original, separate positions into the new and richer understanding that they both now share.

This mutuality does not imply that all religions, anymore than all religious beliefs, are equally valid with nothing to choose between them. Once again we can bring the by now familiar criteria into play including what best seems to `fit` the facts, internal logic and the interests that are being served.

Whilst we need to make up our minds about what we are going to believe and the basis for our actions, final decisions about another religion, especially when it is taken as a whole, are probably neither necessary nor possible for most of us. We certainly need to be even more modest about our conclusions than usual since any proper understanding, let alone assent, involves an empathy which goes far beyond dialogue to something more like jumping out of our own skin and getting inside the skin of the other.

Where religious believers take their beliefs seriously, so that they understand their own identity and can explain it to others, but also carry themselves and their beliefs modestly, it can bode well for community relations. Where they take a more strident attitude a much less promising scenario can develop and often has, marked by intolerance and a crusading spirit. It does not however necessarily follow. Diehard religious beliefs are by no means the only factors which contribute to disastrous community relations. Poverty, marginalisation, injustice and fear can be far more potent (and can themselves contribute to religious intransigence). And there are plenty of examples of Jews and Christians, Moslems and others, all convinced of the God-given truth of their own religion and the inadequacy of everyone else's, agreeing to disagree and living in peace and harmony with each other.

4. A third practical implication of the humanity of religion has to do with its public role. Since the Enlightenment and the spread of secularisation, religion, as represented in the West by the Christian church, has been put in its place. It was seen to be all too powerful and dictatorial in too many realms of life, politics and economics included, and the ascendancy of reason and science made its authority seem much less impressive. Instead of calling the tune, it was relegated within the secular state to the private sphere of personal religion and relationships between individuals and their God. Of late religion has re-emerged in a very public way and religious groups have sought to dictate public policy affecting everyone on the basis of their faith. Neo-conservatives in the US have been highly influential in national (stem-cell research) and international (the `war on terror`) policy-making despite being citizens of a secular state. Nigerian Christians have demanded and achieved the outlawing of homosexual practices. Sikhs and Moslems in Europe have threatened freedom of speech and artistic expression.

There may be several good reasons to question these recent developments but the humanity of religion is certainly one of them. To insist that a religious belief should have prior claim when deciding public policy is to imply that it represents a higher authority than all the other voices clamouring to be heard. It is to claim that it is above the human fray when, according to an understanding of religion as human, it is not.

That does not mean we should make the opposite mistake and exclude religious voices from contributing enthusiastically to the debate. Human as they may be, religious beliefs are full of valuable insights, for example into how human beings tend to behave and how the quality of our lives can be improved or at least saved from the worst. They constantly speak of values that are worth upholding. It would be foolish and self-defeating to ignore what they have to say. In any case they remain the opinions of members of society who have as much right to be heard as the rest.

Religious beliefs however, being human, must contribute to public policy by playing their part in the consensus-building process and not by over-ruling it. They are themselves the outcome of such a process. Ideas about truth and goodness, born out of experience, had to make their way against other ideas and experiences and prove their staying power over long periods of time. Only then did they become apparently settled, though not always accepted, points of view. Now, in what for many is a new public arena where different religious traditions are represented in significant numbers and have sufficient weight to make their presence felt - what we call a `multi-faith` or a `plural` society - they have to submit themselves to the same process again. They must persuade their fellow citizens, including adherents of other religions, of the merits of their case rather than demand that everyone submits to it because, unlike the views of others, it comes with divine authority.

Democracy, the rule of the people or in practice the rule of the majority through an elected, representative government, is far from a perfect political system. For one thing it too easily assumes that all the members of a community can raise their voices and exert their influence in an equally powerful way, which is manifestly not the case. It remains however the best system we know. It insists that at the end of the day the only valid reason for the policies it adopts is that they represent the will of the people. Some of the hottest debates are about whether they do or not. There is no final arbiter short of the ballot box that we can justify except the consensus which people arrive at for all sorts of different reasons as well as shared ones. In building that consensus it will be wise to listen to as many voices as possible in open debate, criticising, correcting and complementing one another as well as compromising as they go along. None of those voices however, whether wise or charismatic or loud or ancient, should override or dictate the emerging consensus. They can and must contribute to it. They have no mandate to override it. They are an essential part of the democratic process but not a replacement for it. Religious voices are no exception.

What is being advocated here might be described as `the re-privatisation of religion`. Originally privatisation meant reducing the influence of religion to the private sphere between a person and their God. It would have nothing to say or be allowed to say

79

anything about public policy. Politics was not its business. `Re-privatisation` fully recognises that religion does have and should have much to contribute to public debate and policy making. It remains `private` however in the sense that its influence is felt by way of individuals and groups openly expressing their `private` religious opinions in the process of consensus building and policy making, but not by way of direct attempts to dictate public policies as such.

5. Finally, what are the practical implications of the humanity of religion for what could be seen as its most important and characteristic activity, namely worship, trailing in its wake calls to undivided loyalty, adoration, trust and obedience?

If God is to be worshipped, God has to be described. This has been done pictorially, despite Old Testament warnings against graven images, but more often by verbal accounts of God's attributes or character, his priorities and purposes and what he requires of us. The convention of assuming that God is a male is itself of course a description. In the Christian tradition God has had a triple personality as Father, Son and Spirit. Sometimes the character of one, as a stern and vengeful judge for example, has appeared to be at odds with that of another, in this case as all-forgiving. God is described somewhat paradoxically in his power and might, his intolerance of sin and evil, his yearning to seek and save the lost, his mission to create and re-create the earth and complete his kingdom. What he requires of obedient worshippers is often spelt out in fine detail with regard to their behaviour towards him and each other. In general he is most often described as Christlike, the known rather than the unknown God of Paul's famous speech to the men of Athens (Acts 17): all loving, all caring, all powerful. In chapter I we touched on some of the difficulties that these descriptions can raise and how there can be significant evidence against them as well as in their favour.

On our understanding of religious beliefs all these descriptions, satisfactory or otherwise, are made by us. That does not necessarily mean that there is no God or that our accounts of God are mere fantasy or wishful thinking and correspond to nothing at all `out there` (or `in there`) in the real world. Neither does it mean that these accounts of God are inevitably misleading rather than thoughtful attempts to put genuine experiences, supposedly of God, into words. It does mean however that what we have in mind when we worship, in other words our image of God, is a human image, limited, relative and easily skewed by self-interest, like the `private` God and the `revolutionary` God and the `male` God we have already discussed or the God who is more or less tolerant according to how we may feel about a particular issue or person. We cannot therefore submit ourselves to this God without reservation.

The idea, central to nearly all religious traditions, that there is only one God and that he or she alone is to be worshipped, curiously leads us to the same conclusion. Since what in practice we have to worship is not God but many accounts of what we think, or want to think, that God is like, we cannot worship them. Religion itself teaches us not to. They are the many not the one. The only way to worship the one God is to worship none of them at all!

Does that put an end to many of the attitudes we associate with worship and often admire in others even when we don't always achieve them for ourselves? Words and phrases like `wholehearted commitment`, `undivided loyalty`, `adoring love`, `complete trust`, `unquestioning faith` and `humble obedience` come to mind. Clearly it does not put an end to them but it does mean that we have to assess their merits and dangers, even their inevitabilities, in a setting where the object of them is human rather than divine. `Undivided loyalty` and `wholehearted commitment` are fine as, say, practical expressions of the rightness of a cause and its need of good, solid support if it is to succeed. 'Trust' and 'faith', which take us further than we might otherwise go, often seem perfectly appropriate responses to the impression a person makes on us

81

because of their winning ways, their knowledge and experience, their apparent integrity or the potential in them which needs to be given a chance to flourish. `Humble obedience` can be a completely understandable attitude towards those we highly respect because of their wisdom and character. Such attitudes are not only acceptable but necessary if life is to go on.

Where they go wrong is when these attitudes `go blind` and cease to remember that people, with their institutions and causes however admirable, are never perfect. The most trustworthy person can conceivably let us down. The wisest leader can make mistakes. What looked like good advice can prove otherwise. Once again a difficult balance has to be struck, or a level of maturity achieved, which makes plenty of room for commitment but maintains a measure not of the cynicism which turns everything sour but of the scepticism which at least remains open to the possibility that commitment or loyalty on this occasion is not entirely warranted.

Whilst much of this is common sense in the everyday world, it may not seem so obvious when supposedly encountering the divine. But whilst God, should God exist (and for me the jury is still out), may be above all such reservations, our `man-made` images of God as the only objects we have to worship, are not.

There is a far more positive side however to this argument. Recognising these images as human, however inspiring, and therefore not to be idolised, not only helps to keep in mind the real possibility that our imaginings may be rather less satisfactory than our adoring attitudes suggest, it also heightens our awareness that there may well be something which transcends them which is rather more satisfactory than we had so far thought of or imagined and to which we can aspire. The humanity of our images of God not only alerts us to the fact that they are less than ideal (even idols at times) but awakens us to the real possibility that there are far better images, visions and values that transcend them. Understood for what they are they point us beyond themselves rather than confront us with journeys end. If they help us to see anything, it is seen through a glass darkly and we shall not mistake the glass for what is beyond it. The attitude we shall therefore bring to worship, whether as congregation or president, is not one of mere acceptance or acquiescence but of scepticism and expectation, not of mere submission but of subversion and aspiration, not of closing down but of opening up, not of knowing but of seeking and searching. To worship is to receive what is given with measured gratitude and respect in order to be stimulated to aspire to what is not. It is to understand that religion and worship have too often been seen as offering certainties rather than as issuing invitations to transcendence: to loyally stop here rather than go further.

Church services, however, need not necessarily or primarily be thought of as acts of worship as we shall now go on to see.

V ON GOING TO CHURCH

1. It is easy to think of reasons for not going to a particular church. We may not get on with the minister (or priest, or vicar or pastor) or the people. It is too big or too small for us. The style of worship doesn't suit us. It is too liberal or conservative. It is just as easy to think of reasons for not going to church in general. A certain level of unbelief is obviously one of them. If we have serious reservations about the fundamentals of Christianity, such as the divinity of Christ, his resurrection from the dead, his sacrifice for our sins, our hope of heaven, even the existence of God himself, then integrity, if nothing else, might keep us away.

Besides these doubts there are plenty of familiar criticisms levelled against the church to add to the disaffection and encourage our absence. High profile scandals dent its reputation. Priests are eventually taken to court for abusive behaviour whilst the church is accused of a cover-up. Women are treated as second-class citizens. Homosexual practices are denounced as sinful and those who practice them are barely tolerated. Christians are wide open to the charge of hypocrisy for not living up to what they believe. They preach peace and reconciliation but are often bitterly and stubbornly divided between themselves. They speak of sacrifice but seem on average to give up very little. They justify being rich in a poor world. Despite high standards their behaviour is not noticeably better than that of the population at large.

At the institutional level the church does not seem to engage very effectively with the issues of the day despite the super-human resources at its disposal. When it comes to gun crime, family breakdown, immigration, community and inter-faith relations, consumerism, financial crises, war, terrorism and climate change the church seems to be no more effective or interested than anyone else. Instead it tends to be wrapped up in its own concerns and internal disputes. It wonders how it can hold together and survive in an increasingly plural and fractured world where religion is suspect. It experiments with new forms of missionary work designed not so much to benefit the evangelised as to increase its own numbers and shore up support. What was originally a daring, outward-going movement has become timid and inward-looking and all too many attend its services, not to engage with a lost and broken world but to enjoy some respite from it.

The case against the church as we know it (the story may be quite different elsewhere, in Africa for example) is easily mounted, though any fair account of the matter should quickly add that the verdict is far from clear. In the face of most of the charges brought against it there is still a good case for the defence. Not every member of the church or every institutional part of it is equally guilty as charged, and in many cases the criticisms are ill-informed and unjustified. In contrast to dwindling congregations many are growing because they are attractive and meet people's needs. For every public scandal there are innumerable quiet acts of sacrifice and love. For every closed door there are plenty that are open and welcoming. If all too many congregations are turned in on themselves there are others busy reaching out in friendship to the communities around them. Large numbers of churchgoing people make up the backbone of anti-poverty campaigns and other movements for justice and social change. Stories of disunity, however true and painful, cannot obscure the determination of many to be reconciled not only with those of their own faith but with those of other faiths as well.

There is then another side to the story. Nevertheless the church's reputation does not stand particularly high and it is not hard to think of reasons for staying away. Some of them, like refusing to attend church in order to get your child into a school, we might even applaud.

2. This discussion however is not about what we should or should not do, given the evidence, but what as a matter of fact we do do and why. To be personal and concrete, it is about what I do despite the extent of my apparent unbelief. As a matter of fact it would now be much easier for me to stay away from church than when, as an ordained minister in charge of local congregations, to stay away (which crossed my mind more than once) would have meant losing my job. So why, when in material terms far less is at stake, do I, along with others whose believing is unsettled to say the least, still turn up?

To begin with there is an undoubted emotional attachment which is hard to break. Many like me will have belonged to the church all their lives. It is associated with events of lasting significance for them and with many rites of passage. It has influenced life-changing decisions they have made. Family and longstanding friends are there so they go for the people if not always for the prayers. The church is valued as a crutch, or a refuge, or a place of respite in times of trouble when the long days get particularly rough. It is where we feel at home and have our place and role to play and are recognised and accepted for what we are. It is part of our identity or self-understanding so that to let go of it would be to let go of a significant part of ourselves. We may be criticised for attending church for what appear to be sentimental reasons but we nevertheless do.

A second reason for still going takes us back to a central theme of this discussion namely `the humanity of religion`. Some may be very disappointed, even offended, that religion has been reduced to such a level. For others however recognising and accepting its humanity can be a relief and help to reconcile them to religion rather than alienate them from it. Many of the problems with religion arise because we expect too much of it. The point is easily made with regard to the church itself since it is fairly easily recognised as a human institution, organised by men and women, governed by them and peopled by them. If it is the bride of Christ it is a very human bride. So why should we be surprised or unduly put out when the church and its associates let themselves down? That is what humans do. Perfection may be on the agenda in some quarters (Methodism for example) and even thought of as

86

attainable, but it is not the church's present state and is not likely to be so in the foreseeable future. That does not mean that we approve of quarrels and scandals, misdemeanours and double standards, but it does mean that we are not thrown totally off balance by them. It is often remarked that Christians are sinners like the rest; better however to say that they, and their institutions, are human like the rest and be rather more relaxed than shocked when it proves to be the case.

Much the same point applies to our religious beliefs. Part of the problem, once again, is that we expect too much of them. When it comes to the deeper problems of life, like suffering and sorrow and loss, we expect them to have complete answers to our fairly predictable but painful questions. When it comes to the enormous mysteries (stretching beyond even the seemingly endless reaches of the universe in both time and space) that surround our lives and make us wonder why we are here and where we are going, we expect them to be all knowing and clear the mystery away. When our insecurities become all too apparent we expect our religious beliefs to supply us with the ultimate reassurance that we are safe and sound, loved and accepted. When things go wrong we expect them to hold the key to putting them right. Or at least that is what we do when we think of our beliefs as from God and above the human fray. Unlike us they are all-knowing. Unlike us they are not compromised or qualified by the changing conditions and fortunes of life. Unlike us they do not tend to say one thing on one occasion and a rather different thing on another. Unlike us they have no vested interests but are completely objective, favouring everyone and no-one. Unlike us, by definition, they can't be wrong.

All of which may be an exaggerated account of attitudes to beliefs, but something of that expectancy creeps in and makes us more troubled than we need to be when cracks and fissures begin to appear in them. Once again it doesn't mean we should not take these fault lines seriously and make our beliefs as coherent as we can by thinking them through and evaluating them in the ways we have already discussed, but we can never turn them into water tight accounts of our life on earth, not even by decamping to some other church where all is fixed and final.

So going to church and finding that a lot of what is said is not entirely satisfactory once you think about it is not the most obvious reason for staying away. To put it more positively, remembering that what is said, however lofty it may sound, is human can make us more relaxed, argumentative and stimulated rather than offended or alienated when we find we don't agree.

A third reason why I still go to church (besides, first, its emotional pull and, second, recognising that my reservations about what is said and done there have to do as much with its human nature as with its failings) is to take advantage of an institutionalised opportunity to be stopped in my tracks, rather like, I imagine, a Muslim submits himself to the daily round of prayer. It is all too easy for life to go on from day to day, week by week, year in year out, as a virtually uninterrupted sequence of more work than play. There is too much to do for it to be otherwise if all our commitments to jobs, families, friends and communities are to be met. The assumptions upon which all this activity is based go unquestioned. With eyes straight ahead or fixed on the ground we scarcely look up or sideways. It is a truism that a healthy life-style involves rest and relaxation and time to stand back and take stock of what we are doing as well as activity. Under pressure, however, the more restful and reflective parts of the package tend to be most at risk.

Regular churchgoing can easily be seen as a duty and even an irksome one with strong over-tones of Sunday or `Sabbath` observance. It might better be seen as a health cure which ensures that we do what otherwise we are very unlikely to do left to ourselves. What we encounter there is not another world since we are still in the realm of the human, but it is another way of looking at the world. It can shed what generations have found to be a very revealing light on it. It raises questions about what it all means and why we are here. It confronts us with a hopeful scenario as well as a stern and realistic one. It challenges our priorities and puts a lot of what we are busy doing into perspective. It suggests what matters and why some of what we do may not matter quite so much as we thought. If we will let it, it does not impose limits (as all too often religion and its authorities are prone to do) but invites us to transcend the limits we have set: to our imagination for example, or expectations, or sympathies or aspirations. A church service or liturgy, with its colourful images, architecture, music, memories, rituals, words and songs , all shot through with beliefs about the length and breadth, heights and depths of our human life, can throw us into the kind of reflective mode which might otherwise elude us. Even if what I see and hear there is open to question, so that I may not agree with the words of a hymn, or the second lesson, or the sermon, it offers a regular opportunity and stimulus to recover a sense of perspective on life in the light of which we may resolve to live differently or persevere in much the same way but leave the church in rather better shape than when we arrived. Of course it is perfectly possible to stop and meditate on life in private, as many do; but for me at least the liturgy of the church and its setting offer far richer resources and, quite crucially, companionable support for what I am not very good at doing on my own.

3. None of these reasons for still going to church however are really sustainable unless there remains something of substance in what I find when I get there. To take an image from the liturgy and the gospels, it is no good interrupting the daily routine to sit at table with longstanding friends if the bread and wine we share is no longer nourishing, or indeed if the wine has turned sour and the bread has gone dry and turned to stone. If what is on offer is not only understandably and inevitably human, with all the qualifications which that implies, but completely unappetising and unsustaining as well, then what purports to be a feast has become a famine and, because I need the nourishment, I had better look elsewhere.

That is why, without attempting to be exhaustive, I need to indicate something of what I do believe and do find sustaining when I go to church and share in a rounded liturgy (or service) of Word and Sacrament, and not just what I don't. Here are four examples.

First I am sustained by the hopefulness of the Christian tradition. It is reflected in its confidence that God's people will find their promised land, that dry bones can live again, that exiles will return, that people can be changed, that love can be crucified but not buried for ever, that dreams of a kingdom ruled by love and justice will come true, that evil in all its forms can be overcome and that a new world can be fashioned.

For me this does not amount to any kind of certainty (`a sure and certain hope`) that at the end of the long day all will be well, much as I would wish it to be so. There is no guarantee that I can find of a happy ending. Nor do I see in it a rather superficial and breezy optimism that always looks on the bright side. And I am suspicious, as we have seen, of identifying my Christian hope with historical progress or a successful campaign or mission where Christianity finally reigns supreme over all mankind.

The hopefulness which sustains me makes two key affirmations. One is that the world and its scenarios are never closed. To put it more mundanely, I believe that there is no situation in life or set of circumstances, including our relationships, in which no more good can be done and nothing new can be created. Not all things are possible but more is always possible. The other is that hope is not so much what we get out of situations, according to whether the signs are favourable or otherwise, but what we put into them. By believing in their potential, especially that of the men and women who inhabit them, and acting accordingly we actually breed hopefulness into them and create possibilities which otherwise might never exist. Hope, as I believe in it, is pro-active, not re-active.

Many a story of men and women setting out `in faith`, as the Bible puts it, determined to change things for the better against the odds, reflect this pro-active kind of hope, but it is constantly evoked for me by two great Christian images. In one, `God` looks out as it were in the beginning on what for the Jews was the frightening spectacle of deep primeval waters without form and void. In the other the `God` we know in Christ looks out on the perhaps even more forbidding spectacle of a world torn apart by our insecurities and destructive behaviour. In both cases `God` might be forgiven for concluding that nothing could be done, but in both cases `God` believes in the potential of the most unpromising people and sets of circumstances imaginable and, by acting in Creation and Incarnation as if a world could be made and re-made, breeds hope into what seems hopeless and opens up a possible future.

When I go to church these powerful images and ideas, which are no less powerful despite my agnosticism, are reawakened in me and when I leave they are a complex presence, difficult to sum up in a word (`formative`, `supportive`, `stimulating`, `provocative`?) as I go on living with others in seemingly intractable situations, from the personal day to day relations to the political, where all too often it seems all too reasonable to give up.

Second, I am sustained by the concern of the Christian tradition for justice, freedom from oppression and, since the poor are usually the oppressed, for the poor. It goes back at least to the Exodus of slaves from Egypt. It is upheld by several of the prophets including Isaiah, Samuel, Amos and Hosea who will not allow the poor to be exploited. It wins a ringing endorsement in Mary's Magnificat at the beginning of the gospel story where the poor will finally be lifted high by the coming Messiah, whilst Matthew suggests that our attitude to the poor may, at the end of the day, be the single most important criterion by which the quality of our lives is judged.

Quite a lot of the talk about justice in the Bible and the tradition which flows from it has of course been interested in moral and legal

91

questions. It sets out the law. It castigates those who disobey it. It asks in what way it survives in an era of grace and forgiveness. It faces up to the penalties of disobedience, especially disobedience against God, and how the requirement of justice for punishment is to be satisfied.

The concern for justice which attracts and sustains me however is more akin to the concerns of modern day `liberation theology` which recognises how political, economic, social and legal systems all too often crush and impoverish the weak whilst allowing the strong to prosper at their expense. The freedom or liberation it looks for is not so much from the heavy punishments for sin which the law and God's righteousness require as from the structures and systems we have put in place to order the world which benefit some whilst oppressing and disadvantaging so many more who are thereby denied their chance to flourish.

There are many occasions when the liturgy brings this concern to the forefront of my mind and stirs my spirits, not least when I hear the so-called Nazareth sermon in Luke's Gospel (ch.4). The core of it is lifted from Isaiah, a prophet as concerned with social justice as any. Towards the end it probably refers back to the idea of Jubilee (see Leviticus 25) which sets out, at least in theory, to right some of the wrongs inflicted by society on landless slaves and debtors. It reads like a manifesto for what is to follow:

> The Spirit of the Lord is upon me because he has anointed me;
> he has sent me to announce good news to the poor,
> to proclaim release for prisoners and recovery of sight
>   for the blind;
> to let the broken victims go free,
> to proclaim the year (the Jubilee year?) of the Lord's favour.

When I go to church the cry of the poor and oppressed for justice and freedom is not all that easy for me to avoid and when I leave it is both an irritant and an inspiration as I confront issues like migrant workers, Africa's economy, fair-trade, international debt and the growing gap in so-called `developed` as well as `developing` countries between rich and poor.

Third, I am nourished and sustained by the struggle within the Christian tradition to become inclusive by accepting and affirming people rather than condemning or diminishing them and shutting them out. I refer to a `struggle` because there is much in the tradition, including the Bible as it is read in church, that sounds decidedly exclusive. Nations are discarded by God and God's people, sometimes brutally, or made subservient and then exploited. Gentiles are despised. Sinners and unbelievers are condemned to outer darkness without reprieve. The gates of the Holy City are firmly shut against anything considered unclean. There is no shortage of outsiders. Again, as we have noted before, the tradition can sound inclusive, willing to embrace the whole inhabited earth, but for dubious reasons. The world wide mission of the church, busy making disciples of all nations, takes on imperial overtones, sweeping up or sweeping aside all its rivals as it makes its triumphant progress.

But when I got to church there is much to remind me of the importance of including people in rather than shutting them out - more in fact than I had imagined before re-reading the lectionary passages. Israel softens its attitude to outsiders. It is hospitable towards the stranger within its gates. It is positive towards foreigners like Ruth the faithful daughter-in-law, Naaman the leper, the widow at Zarephath and Cyrus the deliverer. Isaiah (and Micah) breaks fresh ground with his universal vision which brings peace and justice to all the nations through the costly service of God's chosen people, or at least the remnant of them that is left. The Gospels are peppered with incidents where outsiders are befriended and brought in from the cold: tax gatherers and sinners, lepers and children, Romans, Samaritans and Phoenicians, the poor, the blind, the incurable, a woman `who had a bad name in the town` and another caught in adultery. Wise men from the East can also be part of the story. The welcoming reassurance that `in my Father's house are many mansions`, where there is plenty of room for all of us, is a counterbalance to the severe warnings in the same Gospel about the fate that awaits the unbelievers. The Temple cleansing may well have been a protest against how inaccessible God's house had become. And, as the story of the young church progresses and its message runs like wildfire, as predicted, `to the ends of the earth`, the argument that the Gospel is for the Gentiles as much as for the Jews does not take long to win. What God calls clean we are not to call unclean.

The Christian tradition talks a lot about the forgiveness of sins. There is clearly a legal and penal aspect to it where God is only allowed to spare us the punishment the law requires and we deserve because of the sacrifice of Christ. If nothing else, that warns us against dealing lightly with the wrong that we do. But forgiveness also has much to do with including. It reconciles and mends broken relationships. It brings near those who once were far off. Without ignoring them it does not allow the misdemeanours of a tax gatherer like Zacchaeus to shut him out and deny him forever the chance to entertain Jesus and be part of a more creative enterprise. Disobedient and unbelieving Jews can be regrafted into the vine or the olive tree and prodigals can be welcomed back home.

This struggle to include has never been entirely successful. On the contrary Christians have often been busy excluding one another - and still are - let alone those who don't conform to their beliefs and moral standards. Nevertheless when I go to church I hear plenty of talk about inclusion. Peter's story epitomises much of what it has to say. Amongst his several failings is a cowardly act where he runs for cover instead of standing by his friend and master. It is never treated as if it didn't matter. In fact the seriousness of it is rubbed home at a kind of truth commission where three questions are put about his love and loyalty painfully corresponding to his three denials that he even knew Jesus let alone followed him. But the outcome is not the end of Peter`s involvement in the coming of the

Kingdom. He is, surprisingly, to be the rock on which the church is built and he will feed and take care of the flock of Christ. His `sins` as it were do not rule him out. And if this is how it is to be with those who might be excluded because of the wrongs they have done how much more so with those who are excluded because of wrongs done to them or who have done no particular wrong at all: more sinned against than sinning.

I do not find it hard to hear the echoes of that struggle to be inclusive when I go home from church. It disturbs and moves me and stiffens my resolve in a growing number of encounters, not always welcome, with differences of race, nationality, gender, sexuality, faith, social standing, success, origin, or with those who out of fear, misunderstanding, prejudice or for what are regarded as entirely justifiable reasons, I or others prefer to shut out and away.

The Gospel saying about loving our enemies may have much more to it than a moral injunction. It points to the wisdom of opening up to and embracing what we all too often shun as threatening and hostile. Negatively, exclusion may be wrong or the understandable child of our fears. Positively, inclusiveness may bring benefits that surprise us all.

A fourth example of what I do believe rather than what I don't has to do with costly love. Costliness is an unavoidable theme in the Christian tradition. Many of the characters in the Bible are familiar with it. Faith in God was liable to cost Abraham his only son. Temple rituals cost the lives of countless birds and animals. The servant vividly described by Isaiah in a number of lyrical passages and typified by Jesus of Nazareth brings new life and hope to people at great cost to himself. Real peace of mind is too costly for a rich young man advised to sell everything he has, whilst a tax gatherer accepts the cost and returns his ill-gotten gains with interest. Discipleship turns out to be costly, requiring people to leave homes and jobs and family and survive on very little. As the Christian community gains in profile and ruffles the feathers of the establishment, persecution adds to the cost of faithful commitment. Similar scenarios, in which lives are lost, sacrifices are made, comfort and wealth is given up, people suffer and die for the cause, are repeated from day one until now.

Not all of this expense is for the same reason, nor is it equally justified however well meant. If our wrongdoing for example has serious consequences which are far from easy to put right - costly in other words - I certainly don't believe such a sorry situation requires a costly penalty to be paid just for the sake of it or despite the fact that on some occasions it can be resolved without too much pain or hardship. Costliness is not admirable of itself. Quite the reverse: too many lives have been sacrificed unnecessarily and unpardonably in human history.

Two points however I do find compelling. One is that other-regarding love of this kind is almost inevitably expensive. By nature it is of course generous and self-giving but if it really means doing the best we can for our neighbours, by achieving for them (and with them) the justice, freedom, inclusion and opportunities for fulfilment that we want for ourselves, then the deeper we go into what that entails the more likely we are to meet obstacles that are costly to overcome, whether the cost involves our time and patience, our material and spiritual resources or, as has so often been the case with the great lovers of our world as they stood out against all forms of oppression, our own personal safety.

In the case of world poverty for example, there are strong vested interests: economic, political, religious and social, which benefit from the poverty of others and prefer to keep the world as it is. They will not give way without a struggle, as we have seen again and again on a big scale in Eastern European countries, in South Africa, in Burma, in Chile, Nicaragua, Salvador, Zimbabwe and elsewhere and, since they have power, that struggle will cost their opponents dear. The same is true of attempts to achieve a fairer trading world amidst powerful commercial interests and international financial institutions.

Love is expensive. It may even be validated by the cost involved. If such an idea occurs to me in church it worries me when I leave and begin to realise how often, through gestures and sentiment, charity and passing interests and enthusiasms, we try to love on the cheap.

But there is a second point I find compelling and that is that within this costly love lies creative energy. It is intrinsically life enhancing. That does not mean that all who love in a costly way, by staying in solidarity with those they claim to love through thick and thin and by confronting all their enemies and every obstacle in their path to happiness, will inevitably succeed in what they set out to achieve. For one thing they are not the only factor at work in the situation. Others, even if not openly hostile, may not offer the co-operation that is needed. For another thing, love has to be intelligent as well as full of good intentions. We have to love with `all our minds` as well as with `all our hearts` and, being human, we often get it wrong. So once again there are no guarantees; but I still believe in the creative power of costly love and that, whilst it will not necessarily bring about a new world, there can be no new world without it.

Such a conviction has the potential to be highly depressing and de-motivating given the track record of most of us, but whilst we may be humbled we can also be encouraged and inspired when we come across great examples of costly love such as an Oscar Romero or a Luther King or a Mandela or an Aung San Suu Kyi, or the refractions of it in the less high profile lives of those who love their neighbours; and we can be glad and grateful for its creative power.

Here then are four articles of my creed linked to hopefulness, justice and freedom for the oppressed, inclusion and costly love. I could add more, two of which come readily to mind. Talking of love, I believe in being with people and staying with them, getting inside their world as far as possible, standing by them for better for worse through thick and thin, without necessarily approving of all that they do. We might call it `solidarity` or faithfulness. It is sometimes the best we can do for them. It is not unrelated to Christian ideas about incarnation in which God is thought of as getting inside our skin, is made like us and comes to stay with us, promising not to leave.

I also find the `realism` of the Christian tradition convincing. Put bluntly, it takes a thoroughly pessimistic (more so than in Islam) view of our human nature. It does not ignore its brighter side, often referred to as `the image of God` (imago Dei) in us, that recognises the entitlement to respect of every human being, their equality before God and their ability to be like God in their creativity, generosity and love. There is however a darker side to us which the same tradition calls `sinful` and `fallen`, `original` or deep-dyed. For whatever reasons we are thoroughly egoistic and destructive and prone to use what power we have to act in our own interests rather than the interests of others. This driving self-interest is not going to go away for all the gifts and grace of the Gospel and we will do no-one any good, or act out of love, if we do not allow for it by building in checks and balances whether in the wide world of politics or in our more immediate personal dealings.

4. Having given some examples of what I do believe, a number of things need to be said about them.

First, they make no claim to be the correct understanding of the Christian tradition or even the fragments of it that I have discussed, and there is no obligation on anyone else calling him or her self Christian to agree with them.

Second, I could not easily explain how I have arrived at them. The process is too complex and the influences far too many for that. Having arrived, I can however test them against the by now familiar reference points we have discussed before. I can examine the evidence for them past and present. I can ask whether they `fit` with my experience and whether they make reasonable sense. I can look for their track record and see how widely these beliefs have been held both inside and outside the Christian community. I can talk about them to my contemporaries and open myself up to their constructive critique. The result will not put my beliefs beyond question but it will give them a greater measure of credibility.

Third, these beliefs obviously owe much to my lifelong immersion in the Christian tradition, but they are not altogether unique to it and it is not their only source. Similar insights can be found in other traditions and in any case Christianity throughout its history has interacted with the world around it, with its cultures, religious ideas and secular disciplines, and has not only been affected but has gained much wisdom in doing so. I should add that I personally find some beliefs attractive, in the Buddhist tradition for example, which are not found in the Christian tradition at all.

Fourth, my beliefs are subject to the human characteristics which mark all religious beliefs. They are coloured by self interest and limited by the little that I know compared to what I don't. They are relative to my personality, my experience, the intellectual and social context in which I live and the events that have enriched and scarred my life. Had it been otherwise, I might well have believed differently. Their `partiality` makes it all the more important to keep them open to the stimulus of the `partiality` of others.

Fifth, having made up my mind, I am serious about these beliefs, serious enough to be a bit of an evangelist for them at times and to live with them as best as I know how. Equally, I am aware of their limitations and the need to transcend them.

Sixth, it is often remarked that once we let go of belief in God, in another world, revelation and the divinity of Christ, Christianity is reduced to little more than a set of values. It leaves us with values and principles with which we ought to live by or choose to do so, like being inclusive and loving in a costly way, but it no longer tells us anything about how things actually are: that we are actually loved and accepted by God for example, or that on top of trying to be hopeful we have a sure and certain hope that in the end all shall be well as God sums up all things in Christ and inaugurates God's new creation.

Admittedly we are wary of what Christianity or any other tradition claims to tell us about how things are, given our understanding of the humanity of religion. We have to sort out `how things are` from our experience as best we can. But, if we look at what has been said about what I believe, it amounts to more than a set of values. My commitment to Christian realism is a clear example. It is primarily a wake-up call about the kind of world we live in where self-interest and power are always factors to be reckoned with. It has the flavour of a `fact` rather than a `value`. It talks about what `is` the case rather than what `ought` to be the case, and if we want to be of any use to the world we ignore it at our peril. Other beliefs have a similar flavour. I do not only believe that hopefulness, or inclusion, or costly love are good things and that we `ought` to behave accordingly. I believe they are key insights into how the world works or fails to work and how renewed life, creative energy and undreamed of possibilities are actually brought about. I do not only believe what `ought` to be; I also believe what `is` the case and what will prove to be productive and life enhancing and a source of gift and grace when it comes to moving our sad and sorry world a little nearer to joy. My beliefs are not different from others because they only deal with ethical principles and have nothing to say about the truth of our lives. My beliefs are different from others only in that I can believe them in the face of the evidence to hand, whereas the others I cannot.

5. What then of Jesus of Nazareth who has so far scarcely received a mention in this attempt to be constructive? I have confessed my difficulties when it comes to believing in his divinity as entirely unique to him, but I have no difficulty in revering him as an astonishingly impressive and charismatic figure who really makes a difference, head and shoulders above most if not all others in history. If for me he is not unique as the Son of God he is unique as the paradigm of all that nourishes and inspires me and that I believe to be true when I go to church. For me he exemplifies not what happened once upon a time to save the world from sin but so much of what is happening all the time, before and after his brief ministry, to sustain and renew the world's life.

To me he exemplifies costly love. He suffers and dies on the cross not because some penal theory requires it but as the almost inevitable result of his deep unwavering love for humanity. That love is shown by his commitment to bring about justice for the poor and freedom from oppression as declared in his inaugural sermon, hard as that would be under the weight of the Roman occupation and in a very different political system from our own. That love is shown by his insistence on including the outsider, whether poor or sick or foreign or condemned as a sinner, on every conceivable occasion. The stories and parables that touch on these themes are numerous. They are rehearsed in Gospel readings in church over and over again and produce in the mind's eye a procession of images where the rich are loved but berated, the unemployed are taken on, the Prodigal comes home, the last become first, the untouchable is touched, the lost are sought after and found, the heavy hand of the law is rebuked, the hungry are fed, the banquet is opened up to all comers and the thief finds a friend and a future.

As a result the world of Palestine, which the poor and oppressed wanted to change but powerful rulers and religious leaders wanted to keep much the same, seemed about to be turned upside down. The policies and opinions of the rulers of the Jews were challenged and flouted. The social order could possibly be disturbed. The Temple authorities were severely criticised and undermined. Even the Romans were persuaded of the threat to peace and stability in this outpost of empire. This love, persistent in its solidarity, had come up against powerful vested interests. It rapidly became costly involving not only an uprooted and homeless (though far from joyless) existence, but hostile accusations, sweaty fear, betrayal, arrest, abandonment, torture, humiliation and execution. He suffered and died because he loved.

I find it hard, as I have said already, to believe in the resurrection of Jesus as often depicted, or to see it as a vindication of his sufferings or a confirmation of his victory and ours over sin and death. I am impressed however by the stories and rumours flying about which strongly suggested that Jesus and all his works were by no means dead and buried but had generated so much new life that it justified talk of a new creation.

So the life of this outstanding man not only illustrates how the `hopefulness` which breeds hope into situations and people by believing in their potential can open up fresh possibilities. It exemplifies how love is both inevitably expensive but also creative. It cannot guarantee a new heaven and a new earth, not even when it is as intense as in the living and dying of this marvellous man, but it contains within itself a creative energy without which a new world can never be brought about.

When I go to church the substantial nourishment I find when I get there is above all focused in my image of this man Jesus, open-armed on a cross. He is the paradigm case. He epitomises much of what I believe to be valuable, true, redemptive and creative for our human life:

> In the cross of Christ I glory
> towering o`er the wrecks of time.
> All the light of sacred story
> gathers round its head sublime.

Many of the things that were said earlier about my beliefs must of course be said about this central and dominating image of the crucified Christ, the focus and exemplification of my faith. I do not claim it is the `correct` image of him. It is my image of him. It is not easy to explain the complexities of how it came about, but it can be tested against what others have made of him and supremely against the Gospel stories and what the Christian tradition has made of them. I am committed to what I imagine this man was about but I hope I am open to it being transcended not least because, like all the rest, the image is a human construct.

6. To return briefly to the liturgy or Sunday service, we have discussed the bible readings, hymns and prayers but not so far the Lord's Supper, Eucharist (Thanksgiving) or Holy Communion. Unlike many in the Protestant tradition (who tend to favour 'Word' rather than 'Sacrament'), I find this regular taking and breaking and sharing of bread and wine with thanksgiving especially nourishing. I understand it is what Christians have normally done together when they have met right from the start. For me it is another point at which much of what I believe becomes focused and intensified. It always strikes a note of hopefulness as it offers thanks and looks forward (doing this 'until he comes'), even if, as always, I do not entirely go along with what is said. The bringing of such basic elements as bread and wine to be consecrated to a holy purpose reminds me of another great theme touched on in this book (in chapter II) which has to do with our dependence upon and respect for nature. The invitation to the meal (what Baptists have sometimes referred to as the 'open table') with its reminders of bigger feasts and banquets to come, speaks of inclusion. The sharing of bread evokes images of the hungry and of justice whilst the breaking of it along with the poured out wine speak powerfully of Christ's costly love. That this meal is an occasion of celebration and not a 'wake' supports me in the belief that such love is not inevitably defeated by the powers of this world but is the source of energetic, creative and sustainable life.

I am always disappointed if the service of Holy Communion does not end with the following post-communion prayer which, despite my many reservations, still rings so many bells for me: of hopeful initiatives, of freedom for all, of inclusion and safety, and of the cost and creativity of love:

Father of all, we give you thanks and praise, that when we were still far off you met us in your Son and brought us home. Dying and living, he declared your love, gave us grace, and opened the gate of glory. May we who share Christ's body live his risen life; we who drink his cup bring life to others; we whom the Spirit lights give light to the world. Keep us firm in the hope you have set before us, so we and all your children shall be free, and the whole earth live to praise your name; through Christ our Lord.

7. In this chapter I have explained why I still go regularly to church and I have described the sustenance I can find when I get there (without suggesting, like most of us, that I always do!). It leaves many loose ends some of which I should at least recognise even if I cannot tie them up.

One has to do with whether anything called Christianity or even religion can really stand up once the familiar structure of belief in God and another world has been removed? In my case, can I entertain any hope for humanity or believe in any redemptive and healing processes which renew and enhance human life, without a Christlike God to support and underwrite them. Can there be goodness without a God to guarantee that in the end it will actually do some good. Can there be creativity without a Creator. These are big, important, philosophical questions. Logic or `theo-logic` (theology) might well say: `No ` to most of them. Without a belief in God very little of the rest makes much sense. Some people however, including myself, might be inclined to say: `Yes` and point to the fact that we do actually have a Christian faith with substance despite the fact that much of the dogma has fallen away. In which case it is tempting to ask whether the Emperor has got any clothes?

Second, by way of loose ends, I have not returned to the problem of suffering (though I have written about it elsewhere - in `Poverty and Christianity` published by the SCM Press) despite the fact that for many it is the biggest obstacle to faith. All too often we get hold of the wrong problem however: how can we reconcile suffering with a loving and powerful God, or why has this happened to such an undeserving person like me! It is the wrong problem because it looks for explanations we cannot have; and if we could to any satisfactory extent it would ironically and perversely justify an appalling reality which cannot and should not be justified. There can be reasons for the suffering that crucifies so many but there cannot be good reasons. The problem of suffering is not how to justify it but how to get rid of it. Understanding its causes will help. The kind of realism I am attracted to will warn us against relying too much on unreliable good will when we try to deal with it. Above all we shall find creative ways forward if we believe in hopefulness, justice, inclusion and costly love. But no explanation can explain the problem away.

Finally, what of that other world beyond death and beyond this world whose existence I find hard to believe in, despite my longing for ultimate safety from fear and danger for me and those I care about? That nagging question confronts this sceptic, once again, with the extent of his unknowing. As days go by and knowledge grows, what I still don't know seems more and more to exceed what I do, and ideas of revelation and authority, as we have argued, are no satisfactory way of cutting through it.

A teacher of mine once suggested that religion is best defined, not in terms of God, but as `what we do with the mysterious unknown that surrounds our lives`. I am not sure that he was right since there is little if anything we can `do` with what is entirely or as yet `unknown`. We can however acknowledge that what we do know and try to make some sense of (in our religious beliefs for example) is almost certainly outweighed by what we don't know, and we can respond to this mysterious unknown by respecting it and refusing to rule out what for the time being we cannot rule in.

That refusal not only applies to belief in another world but to belief in God. I cannot in all honesty definitely rule God in. The evidence for God and the so-called proofs of God's existence remain unconvincing. The Christian claim that we know God in Christ is a human claim which for me is rich with possibilities but finalises nothing. But if I cannot rule God in, neither can I definitely rule God out on the basis of contemporary arguments and proofs: for example, that God is no longer needed to create or explain the universe, or is merely a projection of our human longings. They too are unconvincing. Integrity, at least for me, can only lie, not in respect for God and humility before God, but in respect and humility before that `mysterious unknown` that surrounds our lives.

APPENDIX

AN OMEGA COURSE

The course is designed to help Christians sort out their believing by beginning at the other end (Omega rather than Alpha), and building not on solid rocks of revealed truth but on the shifting sands of their experience.

It can be arranged over anything from 6 – 12 sessions.

1. The course might usefully start by sharing what we find difficult to believe. We may confront these problems when we go to church or they may be the reasons why we stay away. The aim would be to get the issues on the table in a frank, open and non-judgmental way: to accept that they exist rather than argue about their merits or try to resolve them.

Use chapter I: `Hard to Believe`, as background reading.

2. In this session, or as part of the first, we look at some of the reasons why we find some aspects of faith difficult.

Chapter II: `Making Faith Fit`, suggests some reasons in sections 1-3 and can be used as background reading.

3. Are there new realities in today's world, like a multi-faith society, that raise problems for faith? Can and should we adjust our faith to accommodate them? Are there ways in which we can make faith more or less immune to attack?

Read chapter II: `Making Faith Fit`, sections 4 and 5.

4. Read chapter III: `Man Made Faith`, and discuss the idea that faith is something we make up. Is that a disturbing idea, a wrong idea, or common sense? Can we accept that our religion is human like ourselves and has the same human characteristics? Some of those characteristics are discussed in chapter III,

sections 2-4. They could be looked at together or be the subject of separate sessions or group discussions.

5. The Humanity of Religion has a number of implications. Some are dealt with in chapter IV: `Treating Religion as Human`:

- section 1 talks about relativism and the need to make up our
                minds,
- section 2 talks about ethical values and moral rules and whether
                they are as solid as they appear,
- section 3 is about inter-faith relations,
- section 4 discusses the place of religion in public debate and policy
                making,   and
- section 5 asks whether worship has any place in `man-made`
                (made by us) religion.

Chapter IV sections 2-5 could be the subject of separate sessions or group discussions.

6. In this session we discuss the church and especially its (Sunday) services and why we do or do not attend them.

Use chapter V: `On Going to Church`, sections 1 and 2 as background reading.

7. In this session participants could be encouraged to `confess` what they do believe and try to write a creed together. Chapter IV section 1 may be of help when trying to assess those beliefs. (If the language of `belief` is unhelpful, this could be a discussion about what people find `nourishing` about the Christian tradition.)

Use chapter V: `On Going to Church`, sections 3 and 5 as background reading.

(An additional session might look at the problem of suffering as discussed in chapter II sections 1, 2 and 6 and chapter V section 7.)

The course could be evaluated by asking whether it has helped us to think through and live constructively with some of the problems of believing, not whether it has resolved them.